Celebration!

Holy Communion:
A Love Story

The Feast of
the Joy of the Lord
in His Bride

James Lindemann

James (Jim) Lindemann

Webpage: lindespirit.com
email: jim@lindespirit.com
Blog: CovenantMusings.lindespirit.com

©Copyright 2010: James Lindemann; All rights reserved
ISBN 978-0-9916866-0-5
Photo Credit: lanakhviorostova, pixmac.com
1405

Other titles by the author:
COVENANT: The Blood Is The Life
Creation's Ballet for Jesus
In the Image of God: Male and Female He Created Them
Living Waters – Baptism: From His Heart Through Ours

RFL & Son, Publisher
541 33 Street South
Lethbridge, Alberta, Canada T1J 3V7
*1303

Flyleaf

Holy Communion – doctrine or relationship? Yes, this Meal is a doctrine. But it is far more. In fact, it is so great that it can take much explanation to describe it. Martin Luther said that the whole of the Gospel is contained within this event, which in itself involves many other doctrines.

That is its dilemma. To do justice to this encounter between the Lord and His Church, large volumes have been written, but what happens is that a powerful act of relationship becomes reduced to simply words on a page. The living, dynamic aspect of this connection can be missed.

How does one accent the vitality and energy in this Sacrament? Ironically through more words! But, by looking through the eyes of newlyweds, hopefully the richness and excitement can be emphasized so that one will never quite see, understand and experience the Lord's Table in the same way again.

The Author

The author, a pastor himself, is the recipient of perspectives, concerns and interests handed down from a long line of pastors in the Lutheran Church, hence his interest and background in such things as the Sacraments, the Covenant, and even the Star of Bethlehem. His Bible Study groups have also contributed greatly in developing these various themes, and now as retirement approaches, this is a good time to gather these thoughts into a more finished form.

Born and raised in New York City, he has come to also value the life in the smaller communities. With his deeply appreciated companion (his wife), their family bulges at the seams with four natural, two adopted, a variety of foster children, and now grandchildren – there is no end to the usually delightful competition for his attention. Perhaps in the coming years there may even be time to pursue his Master's interest in carpentry.

Table of Contents

Preface   vii

1. The Heart of God   1
  Prayer – A Place to Start
    "Packages" of Words? ... Magic
  The Atmosphere of LOVE
    Prayer is Communication ... The Context of Communication ... The "Atmosphere" of Connection-"He Who Searches Men's Hearts ... "The Voice of My Beloved!" ... "My Beloved Responded: 'Arise, O My Beautiful Lamb and Come with Me'"
  Love's Compelling Eagerness for Connectedness
    Enthusiasm ... Your Glory ... Pure Delight ... The Mark of the Relationship

2. The Bridegroom and His Bride   9
  The Bridegroom Leaves
    "This is a Great Mystery" ... Leaves His Father ... Leaves His Mother
  One Life
    He Cleaves to His Wife ... Covenant's Extraordinary Unity ... The Two shall Become One ... The Whole Bride
  They Shall Become One Flesh
    The "Model" of Sexual Intercourse ... Eagerness and Joy
  The Father-in-Law's Welcome

3. The Bridegroom Comes   19
  His Joy is to be Present
    "Jesus Came and Stood in Their Midst" ... "Jesus Himself Came Near and Went With Them" ... "Lo, I Am With You Always" ... Heaven
  Tangible
    "Human, Real, Living" ... Present ... Holy Communion/Holy Community ... Concrete Evidence ... Anticipated for So Long
  With Us – With Him
    1. The Engagement ... 2. The Wedding:

4. The Cinderella Bride   27
  From Rags
    Dinner? ... Let's Brake for Sin ... No Fairy Godmother?? ... No Magic Wand
  From Rags To Palace – The Bride is Won
  The Bride is Made Beautiful
    The Royal Bath ... Beauty Emerges ... The Radiant Bride
  The Blushing Bride

5. This is MY Child!   33
Adoption
> Destined to be His Children ... *God*'s Child ... Joint-Heirs ... My Child, My Beloved

Partakers of the Divine Nature
> Partakers ... "Stuck" With Us–No Back Door ... We Can Reject–The Prodigal Son

We've Only Just Begun

By Grace

6. He Said So   41
Overwhelmed

What is Faith?
> Technical Language ... Faith as Feeling ... Because She Said So! ... Because *HE* Said So!

His Word Depends on Him–Based on His Character

His Trustworthiness–Supernatural For Us
> Not In Our Nature ... The Rebellious Revolutionized

The Power of His Word
> Even When We are Unaware, His Word Still Works ... The Implications of His Word

Sophisticated Faith?
> Become Like a Child ... Must Be an Adult ... Tension Between Faith and ...

The Presence
> Powerful Affirmation of His Word ... Because He Said So

7. Presenting The Bride   51
Company's Coming!
> The Guest List ... Never Alone

A Wonderful and Comforting Connection
> The Place of Connection ... "All the Company of Heaven" ... A Working Reality ... All Around You

The Body of Christ
> An Extraordinary Expression ... Fingers and Toes, Knees and Nose–Individuals in the Body ... Whose Body? ... But Certainly Not With Them! ... The Goal of the Diversity ... Rarely Realized

A "Nasty" Doctrine
> But I Don't Like Him/Her ... No Little Worlds Unto Ourselves ... "Shaking Things Up a Bit" ... At the Pleasure of the Bridegroom

No Frankenstein Here
> Patch Job? ... The Headship of Jesus ... The Still Small Voice ... Non-Artificial Life ... Gifted ... No Vestigial Parts ... Life Both Ways

Participation
> Pick Me! Pick ME! ... *koinonia* ... The Three Sides of *koinonia* ... "All Men Will Know" ... "As I Have Loved You"

8. The Bride *He Loves*   71

  Deniers, Betrayers, Cowards
    St Peter
      Clumsy Faith ... Accommodating Faith ... Denial ... Significance
    Those He Counted On When He Needed Support
      Sleeping on the Job ... *"deserted Him and fled"*–even the "Beloved" disciple! ... Just Didn't "Get It"
    Judas Iscariot – Perhaps a Participant?
      Denier, Betrayer–How Much of a Difference? ... The Sop ... So is Judas at the Sacrament?
    Defective Disciples–Some Grossly Defective
  Who Approves the Bride?
    The Feast of Communion is God's Idea ... Does Jesus Trust His Own Power? ... Welcomed by Jesus at His Table
  What Marks a Participant in the Bride?
    The Basic Requirements ... It is Not That Jesus is Obliged ... One Bride in All the Earth ... We Don't Get to Choose ... *Who* is Denied?
  Stewards of the Mysteries of God
    A Profound Responsibility ... Serious Responsibility (The Dual Effect ... His Word) ... Limited Responsibility ("Doing God One Better" ... The Master's Will ... The Bridegroom's Feast)
  The Welcome Mat
    The Primary Action: To Invite ... Thirsty ... From the Highways and the By-Ways
  The Limited Unwelcome Mat
    A Negative Side ... The Toughest Responsibility ... Denominational Friction ... The Terrible Dilemma
  The Final Responsibility

9. The Reluctant Bride   97

  The Loving Meal
  No Longer the Exuberance of Love
    Someone Moved ... The Bride Moves Away ... Echoes of Adam and Eve
  Reduced Intimacy
    Fear Rules (Wretched)
    Worthy (The Worthy "Unworthy"? ... The Unworthy "Worthy"? ... The Worthy ... Gratitude)
  Renewal
    Confession ... Restoration
  St Paul's Abused Warning
    Shouldn't We Fear This Feast? ... Contexts, Contexts ... Discerning the Body ... Results ... The Unworthy Manner
  Pride Blocks
    Let's Have Lunch ... I'm Not Ready Yet ... The Scarlet O'Hara Syndrome
  Too Often
    "Familiarity breeds contempt" ... How Often?

"Leprosy"
    Insensitivity ... Spiritually Insensitive ... No Good Reason
Enjoyment

10. Tangible Love   115

The Key Nature of Love
    Love *Must* Give Itself ... Tangible Presence ... Love Giving Itself Continuously
Touchable, Substantial Love
    Why Physical? ... "With fervent desire I have desired to eat/with you"
Powerful Imagery!
    Empowering Imagery ... Telltale Imagery ... Concrete Imagery
The Key Nature of the Words
    Imagery or Reality? ... Simple Words ... Symbolic Words
"Is"
    The Significant Word ... The Significance of "Is" With Jesus ("I Am" ... More "I Am" 's)
Uncomplicated Truth
    Spiritual Mystery ... In, With, and Under
Intimacy
    A Loaf of Bread, a Bottle of Wine, and Thou ... The One Loaf
The Cup of Blessing
    "My Cup Overflows" (Psalm 23:5) ... "This is My Blood of the Covenant" ... "This cup which is poured out for you" ... One

11. The Bride Responds   129

Maranatha!
    Oops – There's the Doorbell! ... The King's Attitude ... The Bride's Reaction
She Celebrates
    The Eucharist ... The Preface
The Sacrifice of Praise
    Our Sacrifice ... The Source of Our Sacrifice ..."Through Him/Offer a Sacrifice of Praise"
The Security of His Love
    She Repents ... The Mutual Joy of His Forgiveness
Real Participation
    "In Remembrance of Me" ... Vivid Memory ... Celebrating the Passover ... At Table with the Bridegroom ... Eavesdroppers? ... The Whole Thing
At a Loss for Words
    To Sleep, Perchance to Dream ... Look Who's the Preacher Now! ... The Statement of Need ... The Lord's Death ... Let Go ... He Comes ... Until He Comes ... More to the Death ... Now No Condemnation

12. The Liturgy   **145**
   The Rehearsal
   Leitourgia
      Background of the Word ... The Common Service ... Point/Counterpoint Surrounding Holy Communion
   "Love One Another as I Have Loved You"
      One Another ... Love ... My Brothers
   How Can I?
      In Theory ... "He Said So!" ... Well, Then, I Guess I Love
   The Midas Touch
      A Most Startling Event ... Accountability ... A Consciousness ... The Golden Mundane ... Tarnished Gold
   Packing a Lunch
      Viaticum ... Lunch For On the Go ... "Brown-Bagging It" ... "Go in Peace; the Lord is With You" ... For the Journey

13. He Is Known   **159**
   The Emmaus Experience
   The Breaking of the Bread
   He is Known
   To Know Him Again

Endnotes   **163**

Preface

In some old sermon notes, my father mentioned that since he practiced First Communion as an earlier event to Confirmation, he was invited by a Lutheran congregation to speak to them about this practice. The inevitable question was raised, "Do children really understand Holy Communion?" His answer was to turn the question around: "Do *you*? What do *you* understand?" He found that the replies he received usually spoke of Holy Communion as "receiving IT." He commented that "we will never really begin to understand this Sacrament until we learn to say 'HIM' – *for we receive the Lord Jesus Christ.*"

His insight is most significant. Perhaps theologically we may proclaim this reality, but many seem to not be aware that Holy Communion is a dynamic relationship, not just merely a vehicle by which we receive some *"thing"* – that *thing* being "the forgiveness of sins," or whatever more it may be. Truly, forgiveness has its part to play, but not as the focus, rather it is the result of the *relationship* that is expressed in this event.

It really is ironic that Lutherans should have such a problem. Luther and his co-workers in the Reformation fought many theological battles against the idea that Holy Communion was merely symbolism, and yet where many Lutherans stop is perhaps just barely beyond symbolism. There is no realization that in the words of institution, Jesus is basically saying to each of us, "This is ME, for YOU!" – the whole of Jesus – Body and Blood, not just His gifts – stands at the altar: not just His forgiveness, but His Love for each individual is present and expressed. Here is the reality of "abide in Me, and I in you" (John 14:20; 15:4-5). This is the power behind the dismissal, "Go in peace, *the Lord is with you*!"

Such a transition of perspective will not always come easy, but it will be very much worth the effort. In using the very Biblical model of the wedding feast and newlyweds, there is opportunity to describe this event of Holy Communion and to pursue implications of what this means as a description of relationship. Most often we look at this Communion basically from the human point of view, but where is the acknowledgement of Jesus' point of view? Where have we ever considered the meaning and perspective behind "With great earnestness I have desired to eat this Passover with you before I suffer" [Luke 22:15] – that is, "I have *really wanted* to have this Communion with you"?

Because of my Lutheran background, there are many quotes from Luther, simply because I am most familiar with him. However, what he says in these quotes I believe express solid truths and principles which doubtlessly can be found in many other Church leaders' writings, although stated in different ways and reflecting different perspectives. I humbly beg the pardon of any who wonder why I do not also quote from those sources as well. Probably that will come in a revision, after dialogue with such observers.

I fully expect that there will be dialogue concerning certain points. Some might be just reactionary, but others will have good theological basis. However, my hope and prayer is that we end up seeing more depth in this relationship and come to appreciate even more not just the gifts but the very presence of Lord as He comes to share Himself yet again with us.

I thank Jane Pollock for spotting various flaws, errors and obtuse places in the book, and for keeping me "on my toes" as I write.

Jim Lindemann

August 31, 2012

Postscript:

Likely with varying degrees of accuracy, the Bible quote translations are mine, however there is a heavy dependence on:

The Interlinear Hebrew/Greek English Bible, 4 volumes
    Jay Green, ed., (Lafayette, IN: Associated Publishers and Authors, 1979)

    As well as
The Online Bible computer program (http://www.onlinebible.net)
    Copyright in Canada
    by Larry Pierce
        (11 Holmwood St., Winterbourne, Ontario, N0B 2V0)

    and particularly its modules for
        The Authorized or King James (1769) Version

American King James Version
    Michael Peter (Stone) Engelbrite (True Grace Ministries)
    Placed into the public domain on November 8, 1999.

also its dictionary linking to *Strong's Concordance* numbers and to

    R Laird Harris, *Theological Wordbook of the Old Testament* (Chicago: Moody Press, 1981)

    Gerhard Kittel and Gerhard Friedrich, ed., *Theological Dictionary of the New Testament*, (Grand Rapids, MI: Wm. B. Eerdmans Publishing Co., 1966).

x

1. The Heart of God

Prayer – A Place to Start

"Packages" of Words?

Would it be odd to discuss Holy Communion by first looking at prayer? Not really! Prayer describes the environment from which both it and Holy Communion spring.

Prayer is often thought of as "packages" of words, often starting with "Dear Lord," and ending with "Amen."

> Some "packages" are more nicely wrapped than others (pretty words).
> Some "packages" do not even have time to get wrapped (cry of need).
> Some "packages" contain very important things.
> Some "packages" just contain a quick note or two.

But then how does one "Pray without ceasing" [1 Thessalonians 5:17]? How could one sleep? How could one do any other tasks in the day? While prayer often does indeed include "packages of words," such an interpretation is far too confining to encompass all that it is.

Magic

When it comes to life, humans want predictability and consistent outcome. We want to standardize, mechanize, formalize, automate. If a prayer "works," then we try to repeat the "success." It is no different than the football teammate who is afraid to wash his "lucky Jersey," or the classmate who has to follow the same routine before a test.

This is the foundation of magic and superstition. It is the attempt to gain power by doing, saying, and/or whatever else is felt would produce the desired outcome. Therefore magic insists on exactly the right words, perhaps even the exact cadence, the exact physical position, the exact aids (such as symbols or potion ingredients) and whatever else is determined as necessary. Warnings are given in magic books that the slip of even the most minor detail may mean that not only does one not get the desired outcome, but also that power might be unleashed without any control.

In prayer, where magic requires the correct words, we wrestle whether we should use "Thee," "Thine," and other Elizabethan language. Where magic requires the correct formula, we contemplate whether the complete prayer must follow a certain pattern (for example, the ACTS anagram [Adoration-Confession-Thanksgiving-Supplication] or the Lord's Prayer [either as the "do-all" prayer, or *the* pattern to follow]). Where magic requires the correct position and the correct actions, we struggle with whether to kneel or to stand, and whether to raise or to fold our hands. Where magic requires the correct setting, is our prayer more triumphant in a church or in a "prayer closet"? Where magic requires the correct tools and symbols, we wonder if a prayer cloth or prayer beads might help us be "more successful."

When prayer does not "work," we question whether we were "sincere enough," or had prayed earnestly enough or made the prayer *sound* earnest enough, or had enough faith, or said the prayer enough times, or some other mechanical thing that we must have missed doing, or doing properly, or doing effectively.

The Atmosphere of LOVE

Prayer is Communication

But what really is prayer? It is not a magic formula, but rather, simply, it is *Communication*. However, this is not merely the relaying of information as a newspaper does, rather it is the essential interchange that occurs between two people *who are deeply in Love*.

The Context of Communication

A large proportion of Communication is non-verbal, that is, not words. Just saying the simple sentence: "I am happy" three times, emphasizing a different word each time, can give three different impressions. The way that the sentence ends also has bearing on its meaning – consider the difference between: "I am happy!!" "I am happy." "I am happy??" Although the words are the same, each example's non-verbal part conveys a different message.

Consider another example: suppose the wife may have had a horrible day. The moment the front door opens, her husband asks, "Did you have a bad day today?" She has not yet said a word, yet in her look, in body posture, in deviation from the normal, and in many other ways she has already communicated many things to her Beloved.

Probably during his day her husband may have passed by many people who also have had a bad day, yet he never noticed. What is the difference? He loves her! therefore his attention is focused more closely on her. Subtle clues will be caught, differences in mood will be detected. He looks for more, He notices more, and therefore He recognizes far more than words could express.

The "Atmosphere" of Connection
– "He Who Searches Men's Hearts"

More than merely "packages" of statements, Communication is an atmosphere of connection, an atmosphere strongly governed by Love.

> Likewise the Spirit assists us in our weakness: we do not know for what to pray as we ought, but where words fail the Spirit Himself intercedes with sighs and groanings. And He Who searches men's hearts knows what is the Spirit's mind, because He intercedes for the saints according to God's will. Romans 8:26-27

Why is the Holy Spirit in our hearts? Why is the Lord "searching the hearts of men"? Why is the Holy Spirit interceding, especially on those things where words fail? It is because of Love, because *God yearns to know* – this is the One Who Loves catching all the unspoken cues, noticing even the subtleties, recognizing the hidden yearnings. This is no microscopic examination that comes with a punitive intent, but rather the desire of Love to know the heart of His Beloved.

It is the same kind of interest as the newlyweds have as they eagerly seek out all the nuances in Communication with each other. And since St Paul in Ephesians 5 declares that the marriage verse from Genesis 2 is the mystery of the relationship between Jesus and His Church, then "this newlywed interest" applies to the Bridegroom Jesus who earnestly seeks out from His Bride, His Church, even – and especially – those things that just cannot be expressed in words. His attention is focused on her: passionate to know her joys, her sorrows, her fears, her dreams, her struggles, her disappointments and her triumphs; fervent to know what is *felt* deep in the heart – the groans and sighs of life, not just the words.

His Bride is His "world," she is the one He would die for – in fact, He did just that. He is the Bridegroom Who prepared for their wedding from before the universe existed. His yearning is to truly know His Bride. A major task of the Holy Spirit's presence is just so that this will happen.

"The Voice of My Beloved!" [Song of Solomon 2:8]

Indeed, we live in an atmosphere of prayer. Prayer is going on all the time (unceasing), not because we make some determined effort, but because the Bridegroom from His side is eagerly watching and listening to His Bride's heart, and Communication is happening. Already the Lord, in His extraordinary Love, is unceasing in gleaning every possible Communication from us.

Would not God know about all our lives already? Truly, at times Communication does indeed merely convey information: "the kids have a dental appointment next Tuesday." But the mere trading of facts is not what Love thirsts for: Love wants to see, hear, touch, taste, feel, understand. He wants the interaction, the being with each other always – the *mutual enjoyment* is what He looks forward to. Love seeks the sharing of the *person*, not just of the facts.

Consider why people get married in the first place: they desire more than just a casual meeting where people merely "catch up" on what each is doing. They want to actually *share life* with each other: they want to be there in the ups and downs, holding on to each other, taking their steps together, looking up and seeing their beloved over the supper table.

How Jesus even much more yearns for us to talk to Him, sharing our day, our deepest longings, our wistful plans, our frustrations, our battles, our delights, our celebrations – our worlds. This is not the mere filling in of details, it is that sharing of all we are and all we care about – He seeks the intimacy of our *selves* in particular. What can possibly describe His delight when He hears the sound of His Bride's – our – voice?

"My Beloved Responded: 'Arise, O My Beautiful Lamb[1] and Come with Me'" [Song of Solomon 2:10]

In return, in our Love for the Lord, we do the same: we eagerly, delightedly watch for His Communication with us. We too watch His actions, in both the Bible and in our lives; we too rejoice in hearing His voice in His Word; we delight in talking with Him, sharing with Him, just spending time with Him. This is the source of what worship should be all about – "I was glad when they said to me, 'Let us go to Jehovah's house!'" [Psalm 122:1].

> O God, You are my God; earnestly I seek You; my soul thirsts for You; my flesh yearns for You as in a land without water, dry and exhausted – yearning to see Your power and Your Glory as I have seen it in the sanctuary.   Psalm 63:1-2

Prayer is the Communication of two persons who are very much in Love.

Love's Compelling Eagerness for Connectedness

Enthusiasm

With this understanding of the atmosphere that stands behind prayer, we also can now have a better look at the nature of what Holy Communion is about. The same Love and its eagerness for Communication lie at the core of this Sacrament. This enthusiasm is captured in Luke 22:15, when Jesus says to His disciples, "With great earnestness I have desired to eat this Passover with you…"; and in our response as in Psalm 63 above: "yearning to see Your power and Your Glory as I have seen it in the sanctuary."

So why is *this* Passover celebration so special as opposed to the others that Jesus and His disciples have shared in the past? Because in this one, the Bread and the Wine would be dramatically altered for the rest of time, when Jesus says, "This is My Body … This is My Blood" – this is ME! – I share My very Self totally and completely with you.

Your Glory

Psalm 63's "Your Glory" deserves a special note here. God's Glory encompasses many things, but of particular interest is the dialogue between Jehovah and Moses in Exodus 33:8-19, where in answer to Moses' "Show me Your Glory," Jehovah says,

> "I will make all My goodness pass before you, and will proclaim before you the [Covenant] Name 'Jehovah'; I will be gracious to whom I will be gracious, and will show mercy on whom I will show mercy …."

God declares that essential characteristics of His Glory are His goodness, His Covenant relationship, His grace and mercy; and then in chapter 34:5-7, He adds His Steadfast Love, faithfulness, forgiveness and justice. This has important considerations for the Psalm 63 quote, since we need to ask just what the "Glory" is that we observe "in the sanctuary." So often we immediately think of His power and majesty (as in Isaiah 6:1-8's and Ezekiel 1:26-28's visions of heaven), but by God's own definition in Exodus, the language is far more relationship-oriented.

This view of His Glory is the starting point when considering Holy Communion, because in what more powerfully concrete form could the Bridegroom demonstrate the Glory of His relationship than that in which He presents His very self and all which it contains to His Bride? It is the astonishing gift of His total self.

Pure Delight

Is this not the essence of the Biblical concept of marriage? It is the sharing of the Bridegroom's fundamental nature with His Bride – it is the very same atmosphere that prayer has! Here is the extraordinary Love that seeks deeper Communication – Communion – with the Beloved, within the pure mutual delight of the Bridegroom with His Bride. Truly this new level of Communication is not initiated by the Bride, but rather by the earnest, eager desire of the Bridegroom. And the response of the Bride is not indifference but to passionately crave what the Bridegroom seeks and offers.

The Mark of the Relationship

The Bridegroom's overwhelming, selfless Love is the mark of Holy Communion – holy Communication. This is the gift of the Bridegroom to His dearly Beloved, His died-for Bride. This is the pure joy of God to have this relationship with His People. This is the very heart of God, His passion, His earnest hungering and thirsting, His Communication. His dying wish is to have this connection to His Bride – a wish made the more powerful by His resurrection.

2. The Bridegroom and His Bride

The Bridegroom Leaves

"This is a Great Mystery" [Ephesians 5:32]

> Therefore a man leaves his father and his mother and cleaves to his wife, and they become one flesh.   Genesis 2:24
>
> the mystery of this is great, and I speak concerning Christ and the Church.   Ephesians 5:32

In Ephesians 5, St Paul identifies that the marriage text from Genesis is actually a prophecy of Jesus and His Bride, and in verses 22-30, he compares husband and wife to *the* Bridegroom and His Bride (the Church), rather than other way around.

It is like the name for a certain door model. As a child, this writer was told that the six-paneled door, where the top two panels are smaller than the rest, was by some called "the Cross and the Open Book." The center wood between the upper four panels forms a cross (as emphasized in the picture), while the bottom panels, especially with the molding outlining the bottom panels, represent an open book. The name reflects the passage where Jesus said: "I am the Door: if any man enters in by Me, he shall be saved …" [John 10:9]. It is not that Jesus is like a door, rather it is that a door represents *the* Door. Every door that we "enter in" reminds us that we must enter through Jesus to receive God's salvation.

Similarly, in verse 32 above, Paul indicates that there really is only one basic Marriage to which the Genesis passage points, all others are simply to be reflections of *the Original*. Within that consideration, looking at marriages around us may give us clues and reminders of the relationship between the Bridegroom and His Bride: if the marriage is good, then we capture an inkling of what are the good things of the perfect relationship; and when the marriage is not good, of those things for which we yearn.

"Leaves His Father" [Genesis 2:24; Ephesians 5:31]

> Christ Jesus, Who, though already in the nature of God, did not clutch at being equal with God, but "neutralized" Himself, taking the nature of a slave, having become the likeness of men.   Philippians 2:5-7

Just as Adam declared/prophesied in Genesis, this Son "leaves" – turns away from the throne of God, puts aside the glory of heaven, leaves His Father, "'neutralizes' (empties) Himself," to become a human – why?

The marriage verse sets a context of our Lord's coming to earth: not only has He come to die to save us, it is also that the Bridegroom comes to win His Beloved, to share Himself and all He is with her. Even today He comes to spend very personal time with His Bride every week. He seeks to become one with her, so that she can become one with Him. This is no mere "arranged" match, where the future couple may only vaguely know about each other and preparations are done by others, instead this is one for which the Bridegroom has planned and worked from before the creation of the world. Therefore comes the eagerness of the Bridegroom, as echoed in Jacob's eagerness after working 14 years for the hand of Rachel [Genesis 29].

"Leaves His Mother" [Genesis 2:24; Ephesians 5:31]

> Jesus said to her, "O woman, what is that between you and Me? My hour is not yet come." John 2:4

At the Wedding of Cana, Jesus breaks His tie of being subject [Luke 2:51] to His mother – politely, respectfully, yet also firmly, identifying that His commitment now lies elsewhere. This is an important action, since there will be times when His mother will be in conflict with His wooing of His Bride [Mark 3:31-35][2]. It is not that he no longer loves and cares for her – even as He dies, He guarantees that she will be taken care of [John 19:25-27], interestingly by the only disciple that will die "naturally" in old age.

Is it not intriguing that it is at a wedding where He leaves His mother, and where He embarks on His ministry, in which He begins the wooing of His Bride? It is just like how many other marriages which have their start when the couples first meet at a wedding!

> This beginning of His signs Jesus did at Cana in Galilee, and revealed His Glory; *and His disciples believed in Him.* John 2:11

His Bride would now become His focus.

One Life

"He Cleaves to His Wife" [Genesis 2:24; Ephesians 5:31]

> "For better and for worse, for richer and for poorer, in sickness and in health, to have and to hold from this day forward until death do us part." From a traditional wedding ceremony

> ...for He Himself has said, "Never will I leave you, never will I forsake you." Hebrews 13:5

> Do not fear, for I am with you, do not search to and fro, for I your God will strengthen you – yes, I will help you; yes, I will uphold you with My righteous right hand.   Isaiah 41:10
>
> For I am confident that neither death, nor life, ... nor what is present, nor what is coming, ... nor any other created thing, will be able to separate us from the Love of God in Christ Jesus our Lord.
>   Romans 8:38-39

Throughout His ministry, seeking His Intended with patience and Love, He reveals Himself: His Nature; His heart; His concerns; His dreams, hopes, and plans for her future. No idealist, He defines Love's cost: for both Himself and His Beloved, there will be struggle to make it through this world, and there will be death. But He will cleave to His Bride even when she turns her back on Him, when she does not trust Him, when she does not understand Him – still He continues to be faithful. There will also be a resurrection – His cleaving reaches beyond death, all the way into new and eternal life –; and when the Marriage Feast commences, she will have an irrevocable place by His side forever.

Covenant's Extraordinary Unity

> For all the fullness of the Godhead dwells bodily in Him...
>   Colossians 2:9

The foundation of "Blood Brother" and any of the other ways in which the relationship of Blood Covenant is identified worldwide, speak not of "contract" but of extraordinary unity – one Blood, one Soul, one Life theoretically flows between two persons. Yet throughout the history of Covenant this oneness has been only in *concept*, not in *concrete* reality – the two so united have not *really* been one.

However, that changes with the birth in Bethlehem: everything that Covenant has been describing since Adam and Eve now literally stands on this earth with two legs. In Jesus, two have truly become one, God and Man are irrevocably united with one Blood, one Soul, one Life. Cut Jesus and Man bleeds, but so also does God![3] Kill Jesus and Man dies, but so also does God![4] "The fullness of the Godhead" indeed dwells bodily in Him.

"The Two shall Become One" [Genesis 2:24; Ephesians 5:31]

> and you also have fullness[5] in Him, Who is the Head over all principalities and authority.   Colossians 2:10
>
> ... the Church, which is His Body, the fullness of Him Who fills all in all.   Ephesians 1:22-23

St Paul continues this universe-shattering concept of "fullness" to also describe Jesus' relationship with his Bride. Here also is a true oneness, but more than a joining of Souls, there is a oneness of Spirit with the Holy Spirit, Who through Baptism dwells in the heart of the Bride; and, beyond symbolism, as the Bread and Wine of Holy Communion becomes one with the physical body, Jesus is made one Blood, one Body with His Bride. Using a slightly different picture, Jesus says:

> Remain in Me, and I in you. As the branch cannot bear fruit of itself, unless it remains in the vine, neither can you, unless you remain in Me. I am the Vine, you are the branches – he who remains in Me and I in him, he bears much fruit, for apart from Me you can do nothing.
>   John 15:4-5

Not only is life experienced together, but the Bride is fulfilled and empowered. Like a married couple who begin to look like each other, the commonality of their lives etches the same laugh lines, the same tear stains, the same concern wrinkles. The Life of the Bridegroom flows throughout the Bride – His Life is her life, and her life is His Life. To separate them would literally mean death.[6]

The Whole Bride

> For He is our peace, Who made us both one ..., that of the two He might create one new human in Himself, so making peace.
> Ephesians 2:14-16

The union within this "walking" Covenant involves not just God the Son with human nature, not just Jesus with His Bride, but also all who make up the Bride: those who are God's special People from the Old Testament background, and those who are the new People of God with the New Testament background – all who are within the Bride are also united with each other and therefore there is one Blood, one Life – and one Flesh (or one "flesh and bone" [Genesis 2:23; Ephesians 5:30]) – between them all.

Truly, this oneness within the Bride may *seem* more conceptual than concrete, yet even now the unity of the Holy Spirit and the presence of Jesus in the heart is real. This is the common link which calls us to jointly pay attention to the will of the Bridegroom, especially in how we treat ourselves, each other, the Church, and the world.

They Shall Become One Flesh

The "Model" of Sexual Intercourse

"Intercourse" – the meaning of the word is: *Dialogue*! A conversation over a cup of coffee in a restaurant is *verbal* intercourse. By its very name then, it has long been recognized that *"sexual* intercourse" is intended by God as a key method of *Communication*; a *language* designed as the expression of Love in the giving of one's self, and the receiving of that gift from the other, within the environment, security and freedom of marriage – a language so designed because words are simply inadequate. The Biblical book, Song of Solomon, describes such deep, personal Communication of Love within God's framework.

This is the intimacy of the heart – which is reminiscent of the Holy Spirit's work as He dwells in our hearts, spoken of in the last chapter. Sadly, our modern age no longer understands that this is Communication, since it focuses on the mechanics of the sexual act and on one's own gratification – a by-product of the selfishness of sin – rather than it be a heartfelt committed gift to one's beloved. By comparison, many have the opinion that worship primarily is the Bride pleasing herself (for example, "I didn't get much out of the service this morning"), when "worship" actually is to proclaim *the "worthy-ship" of the Bridegroom* in His expression of His Love, and to express *her heartfelt committed gift of herself and her life to Him*, with the focus on pleasing *Him*.

Within this context is Jesus' "This is My Body, This is My Blood" where He earnestly, delightedly, boldly, actually, gives Himself "body and soul" – giving literally everything, holding back nothing – to His Bride, seeking her contentment in His Love, and desiring that she would give nothing less than *her* whole self in return.

Eagerness and Joy

Sometimes in the past, sexual intercourse was treated more as an obligation and a duty. But the Song of Solomon describes the passion, the yearning, the eagerness and the delight of this unifying Communication.

So also has Holy Communion sometimes been treated more as an obligation and a duty. As with prayer, we tend to mechanize it. Rules and tradition dictate preparation, frequency (for example, "the less, the better"), and other such customs.

But where is to be found the extraordinary, eager, joyful outpouring of self by the Bridegroom toward His Beloved, an outpouring defined by Love and not by customs? Where do we reflect:

> For as a young man marries a virgin, so shall your sons marry you, and as the bridegroom rejoices over the bride, so shall your God rejoice over you.
> Isaiah 62:5

As St Paul identifies the marriage verse as describing Christ and His Bride, how should we understand the extraordinary elation and zeal that Jesus has in giving Himself to us? The Bridegroom withholds nothing, not His Body, not His Blood – this is His desire, His choice, His extravagant relationship of Love – His joy.

The Father-in-Law's Welcome

> But God, being rich in mercy through His great Love with which He Loved us, even when we were dead in our trespasses, made us alive with Christ (by grace you are saved), and raised us up with Him, and *seated us in the heavenly places in Christ Jesus, that He might show in the coming ages the surpassing riches of His grace in kindness toward us in Christ Jesus.*
> Ephesians 2:4-7

If you think the Bridegroom is eager, just look at His Dad: "Now sit right here next to Me and your Bridegroom – have I got things to show you!"

It will take Him an eternity to show the Bride everything – wonderful things! And it will not be the same kind of eternity as watching merely the family slides (except for those cute, embarrassing ones of Baby Jesus in Bethlehem… [Aw, Dad!!]). Obviously it is inconceivable that the Father regards the Bridegroom and His Bride other than absolutely together – of "one flesh" – even when it comes to the very throne of God.

And St Paul speaks as if all this is already an established fact.

3. The Bridegroom Comes

His Joy is to be Present

"Jesus Came and Stood in Their Midst" [John 20:19]

> For where two or three are gathered in My Name, there am I in the midst of them. Matthew 18:20

Notice – no limitations! Not: "I may come once a month; if you want any more than that, then you'd have to have a good enough reason (but check first with My appointment secretary)." In fact, He does not even say, "if two or three call on Me," as "When he calls on Me, I will answer him" (Psalm 91:15). Rather if they are gathered, then He is right there with them. As the saying puts it: Jesus has no problem "just hanging out" with His Beloved.

"Jesus Himself Came Near and Went With Them" [Luke 24:15]

> Jehovah, You have searched me and known me. You know when I sit and when I rise; You *understand* my thoughts from afar. You assess my path and my lying down, and You are acquainted with all my roads. Not a word is on my tongue but, O Jehovah, You know it all.   Psalm 139:1-4

All the commotion about Jesus "rising from the dead" is just too much hysteria for two disciples. They decide to just go home to Emmaus and wait for it all to die down [Luke 23:13-36]. Yet even on the way they cannot help discussing the events of that day.

These are "two gathered in His Name." They have no thought of "calling on Him" – after all He is dead. Yet Jesus anticipates their need that He should be with them.

How could He even predict their need for His presence? Because the Bridegroom's full attention is turned toward His Bride, to recognize her necessity, and His desire is to be with her. This is what that atmosphere of Communication is all about! The Bridegroom deliberately notices the unspoken cues, the unspoken needs. Even if they have no intentionally planned "business" to do with Jesus, that is not the issue. There is joy to be had even just in the company of the Beloved.

"Lo, I Am With You Always" [Matthew 28:20]

> Such knowledge is a profound mystery for me, it is an understanding I cannot attain: where can I go from Your spirit? or where can I flee from Your face? If I ascend to heaven, You are there; if I spread my bed in Sheol, behold, there You are! If I take the wings of the morning and dwell at the ends of the sea, even there Your Hand shall guide me, and Your Right Hand shall hold me fast.   Psalm 139:6-10

A couple sits in the same room reading their books, and may say little to each other all evening. Yet there is a pervading comfortableness that they share. They just *enjoy* the company of their beloved. Would this Bridegroom and Bride be any less? Again, the key is that atmosphere of deep Love that permeates the relationship of the Bridegroom with His Beloved.

How should we understand Matthew 28:20 ("Lo, I am with you always") and similar passages, except that the Bridegroom is speaking these words to His Bride? Therefore in the context of Love, they are no mere dry words of reassurance, but the pledge from the heart which echoes in the Wedding ceremony: "to Love her, comfort her, honor and keep her, in sickness and in health, and forsaking all others, keep yourself for her only, for as long as you both shall live [forever!]." Again, unmistakably, the Bridegroom wears His heart on His sleeve, for His Beloved to constantly see.

Heaven

> I heard a great voice from the throne saying, "Behold, the dwelling of God is with men. He will dwell with them, they will be His People, and God Himself will be their God with them;   Revelation 21:3
>
> My dwelling shall be with them; and I will be God to them, and they shall be a People to Me.   Ezekiel 37:27

So also these passages give us pause. Often we glide over them without a thought, yet they are dramatically opposite to how we often think of heaven. We see heaven as when finally *we* get "to be with God," but the great Jehovah says, "*My* dwelling place shall be *with them*" – *He* is excited in that *He* gets to be *with us*! It is startling to consider just how much the Bridegroom anticipates finally being able to live forever *where His Bride lives* – which means that the anticipation is mutual!

Tangible

"Human, Real, Living"

> Some may complain that all [the doctrine about God's Love] is too theological, too dogmatic, and perhaps too abstract. Is there not some spot on earth where this great truth can be focused, where we can reach out to this mystery which the angels desired to behold? Can we not have it human, real, living? It is possible.   Berthold von Schenk[7]

In the previous section, that eagerness of God to dwell where His People live forms the foundation for Christmas, where the Bridegroom demonstrates in concrete form His commitment of "withness" – or "Immanuel" ("God with us"). Already, long before the "heaven" of the last section, He personally enters into the Bride's life completely at where she must spend her day. He experiences everything just as she does. She knows that He recoils in horror at nothing that has touched her life. Because of this, she knows that there is nothing she cannot discuss with Him. She has full confidence that He does understand:

> For we have a High Priest, not one who is unable to suffer with us in our weaknesses, but One Who has been tested in all things just like we are, yet without sin – therefore we should approach with confidence the Throne of Grace, that we may receive mercy and find grace for timely help. Hebrews 4:15-16

Present

> [Easter] meant continued, uninterrupted fellowship with Him. Even death was not able to separate them from Him. It meant a companionship that stretched out through life, beyond the grave, into endless eternity. ... We know that our Christ lives, for He lives in us. His living Presence is the joy and comfort of our lives.
> Fred H Lindemann[8]

How does the Bridegroom keep reassuring the Bride that He still is part of her life, still with her? Obviously by constantly being wherever she is found. In concrete reality He affirms again and again that, whether in the Siberian cold or the hot Australian sun, whether in the inner city or with the migrant picking fruit, whether in a stately church or secretly huddled in a house, He is there by her side literally "in flesh and blood" – in His Body and Blood. It is her continuous reminder that He has not forgotten.

Holy Communion / Holy Community

> For exactly as the body is one and has many members, and all the members of the body, being many, are one body, likewise it also is with Christ. For in one Spirit we all were baptized into one Body – whether Jews or Greeks, whether slaves or free men – and all were caused to drink of one Spirit… If one member suffers, all the members suffer with it; if one member is glorified, all the members rejoice together – and *you* are Christ's Body and members sharing in it.
> I Corinthians 12:12-13, 26-27

What's more, the Bridegroom surrounds His Bride so that she does not have to go far to find Him. He enters into every Christian who communes and therefore the reality of His presence is all around and in His Bride. His Beloved voice will speak through one person, His caring help will come through another, His loving comfort through another, and so forth – all are the Bridegroom's active demonstration that not only He is in their midst but also is found *in them*.

Concrete Evidence

What would be better for the Bride that covers the earth but to have a way by which the Bridegroom could *prove* Himself present in every locale simultaneously? That way is through the physical, tangible elements of Bread and Wine; and the physical presence of the Body of Christ all around us! Holy Communion is indeed a masterful solution to the need that would always be here throughout the centuries after Jesus' Ascension – and it is the Bridegroom's idea, not some human scheme. Here is *His* calculated ceaseless proof, always available, that He will never depart from His Beloved. He deeply desires that she know that He is with her, so that she need never despair, never doubt.

Anticipated for So Long

> the mystery which has been hidden from ages and from generations, but now has been revealed to His saints.   Colossians 1:26

This is no grudging, reluctant activity. This has always been the Plan, right from the beginning: to throw Himself, body and soul – Body and Blood[9] – into this personal connection with His Bride.

> The Word became flesh and dwelt among us, and we beheld His Glory, the Glory as of the only begotten of the Father, full of grace and truth.
>   John 1:14

The Bridegroom has no thought of being stingy with Himself, as if He were available only once a month or four times a year. As newlyweds want to constantly be with each other, because such is their Love, so also the Bridegroom would be no less toward His Bride – "wherever two or three are gathered …" This is the *eagerness* of His Love toward His Beloved!

With Us – With Him

His desire that we be together has never diminished, even after all these centuries. In fact, it is building to a climax as He anticipates the day when He will take His Bride finally home. In the culture when Jesus walked the earth, marriage consisted of two stages which have a fascinating parallel to the relationship between this Bridegroom and His Beloved:

1. The Engagement

The prospective bridegroom settles with the father of his intended bride a "Bride Price," which has come to be thought of as an honorable way to thank the parents for raising this young woman. Some parents simply turn this sum over to the daughter as a dowry. [10]

So also Jesus' Bride is "bought at a price" [I Corinthians 6:20; 7:23], "...God's Church which He purchased with His own Blood" [Acts 20:28], and yet this precious price is given to the Bride – us – as our "dowry": "The Cup of Blessing which we bless, is it not participation in Christ's Blood?..." [I Corinthians 10:16].

The hopeful suitor presents to his intended a document (*Ketubah*) describing his promises to his beloved. When she accepts his proposal, she will keep the *Ketubah* until the wedding – as does Jesus' Bride in His written promises, the Bible:

> His divine power has given to us all things which pertain to life and godliness, through the knowledge of Him Who has called us to His own glory and virtue; through which He has given exceeding great and precious promises to us: that through these you might be participants of the divine nature... II Peter 1:3-4

With the promise to prepare a place for his bride, the bridegroom returns to his father's house to build a suitable marriage dwelling for themselves.

> In my Father's house, there are many dwellings; if it were not so, would I have said to you that I go to prepare a place for you?
> John 14:2

Of course, that he has returned to his father's house does not mean that he cannot see his beloved in the meantime. There will be times spent together, gifts and other tokens of Love that will be exchanged.

This engagement is tantamount to marriage, with perhaps the main difference being that during the engagement the couple does not yet live together. So should a child be born during this time, it is considered legitimate – just frowned on that they "could not wait," as is likely the opinion in regard to Mary, "[Joseph's] betrothed wife, who was with child" [Luke 2:5]. And just like marriage, the engagement needs a divorce-like procedure to end it.

2. The Wedding

> But if I go and prepare a place for you, I am coming again and will take you to Myself, that where I am you also will be.   John 14:3

The marriage could occur only after the bridegroom's father is satisfied that his son has skimped on nothing and that all has indeed been prepared. Until that time, when one asks the son about the wedding date, he can only reply that his father alone knows.

> But of that day and the hour no one knows, not even the angels in heaven, nor the Son, but only the Father.   Mark 13:32

It is part of the festivities that the bridegroom comes suddenly. As he and his attendants make their way to the bride, the shout would go up "Behold, the bridegroom is coming; go out to meet him!" [Matthew 25:6]. The excited bride would don her wedding dress, complete her final preparations, and then she and her attendants would go out to meet the bridegroom.

Let us rejoice and jump for joy and give the Glory to Him, since the marriage of the Lamb is come, and His Wife has made herself ready.
Revelation 19:7

Now the couple will live together in their home in the fullness of their marriage. Holy Communion will only intensify on the Last Day!

4. The Cinderella Bride

From Rags

Dinner?

> For the Lamb which is in the midst of the throne shall shepherd them, He shall lead them to Living Fountains of Waters: and God shall wipe away all tears from their eyes. Revelation 7:17

Before all creation, before the powerful holy angels, before all the Heavenly Court, the Bridegroom takes His Bride by the hand and leads – us! – to the Head Table, His Table, the Lord's Table; to be at His side, there to personally feed us as nowadays a bridegroom feeds his bride the wedding cake. Bold and proud is He to have us at His Table.

Let's Brake for Sin

"I brake for yard sales" is a bumper sticker that indicates the driver's interest. When a yard sale comes along, this person will stop and investigate. We have that same propensity with sin. Too often when sin provides an opportunity, we are quick to slam on the brakes to get a better view and perhaps to browse a bit among its wares.

What is sin, anyway? To give an example, how often when we are about to do something wrong, somewhere along the line the thought flashes through our mind that this is indeed wrong? Likely every time, if we look closely enough. But we have made up our mind that the "benefits" (which most often backfire and often turn into a slavery rather than a blessing) cannot be passed by.

So despite knowing better, we go ahead anyway. Sin is not a mistake or an error. It is *intentional rebellion*. That is why Satan has Eve recall the command of Jehovah (Genesis 3:1-3); he is not interested in merely a blunder or a lapse of memory – he wants outright revolt. And he is not interested in us merely tripping – he wants us to *refuse* to follow God's will.

Is *this* the Bride that Jesus proudly takes to dinner – this Bride who has been so intent on rebelling? *This* is the Bride that He would die for? He really must have some kind of Love!

No Fairy Godmother??

There is no fairy godmother in this story to make the Bride beautiful. There are not even attendants to prepare her for the Marriage Feast. In fact, she does not even prepare herself. Unlike the fairy tales, the Bride is not first made beautiful, and only then will the Bridegroom fall in Love with her. In fact, she is not even interested in such a relationship!

> God asserts His Love for us in that while we were *still sinners* Christ died for us. … while we were *enemies* we were reconciled to God by the death of his Son … Romans 5:8, 10

– while she is still in the gutter, already the Bridegroom has Loved His Bride.

No Magic Wand

There is no simple "speak a few words and poof! the Bride is now beautiful." To take His Bride requires that debts be paid, and paid in full, or else she would never belong to Him. It is a steep cost that she – we – could in no way pay:

> A brother cannot at all redeem a man, nor give to God a ransom for him – for costly is the redemption of their Soul … Psalm 49:7-8

The Bridegroom must pay life-for-life in order to free His Bride from the debts of her sin. Is it worth the risk to go so far for a Bride who is not merely uninterested in Him, but rather in active rebellion? What if He "does all," and she still is indifferent? In fact, He does die for many who merely just ridicule or ignore Him. Indeed, He knows what it is like to be "stood up." The cross is no magic wand.

From Rags To Palace – The Bride is Won

But many *are* drawn to Him because of what He has done. In wonder His Bride considers herself and cannot grasp why the Bridegroom chooses her, why He so willingly makes such a *dear* payment – an *expensive* payment, but also such a *cherished* one. But it does not matter that she does not understand – the fact is that He does it.

> He saved us and called us with a holy calling, not according to our works, but according to His own purpose and grace, which have been given to us in Christ Jesus before times eternal. II Timothy 1:9

The Bride is Made Beautiful

The Royal Bath

> Husbands, Love your wives, just as Christ Loved the Church and gave Himself up on her behalf, that *He* might sanctify her, having cleansed her by the washing of water with the Word, that *He* might present to Himself the glorious Church, without spot or wrinkle or anything like

that, but that she might be holy and without blemish.

Ephesians 5:25-27

Trusting the work to no one lesser – in fact, no one else could do it – He prepares the Bride for the Wedding Feast. He takes her by the hand and sets about to clean her up. In loving care, *He* washes her "with the water and the Word." It is His desire and joy to prepare her – it is by grace alone. He does not merely give her "the water and the Word," with instructions to clean herself up. This is at *His* initiative: "according to His mercy He saved us" [Titus 3:5], "because He first Loved us" [1 John 4:19] – it was not *her* idea.

Beauty Emerges

He Himself scrubs away, and behold, what beauty emerges! The scarred, even downright ugly places in the Bride are not just cleansed, but actually are changed: the callused becomes soft; the decayed places rebuilt; the emptiness is filled – the Bride is created anew. All the painful spots He tenderly addresses, the stings and bruises that must be healed.

> ...to give them beauty* instead of ashes, the oil of mirth instead of mourning, the wrap/robe of praise instead of a heavy spirit; that one calls them oaks of righteousness, the garden of Jehovah, in which *He* will be "glorified"* (beautiful).
> Isaiah 61:3 (* = basically same word)

The Radiant Bride

> "I passed over you and looked on you, indeed your time was the time of Love; so I spread My robe over you and covered your nakedness. I swore an oath to you and entered into a Covenant with you," says the Lord Jehovah, "and you became Mine. I washed you in water; I cleansed away your blood, and I anointed you with oil. You I clothed in

embroidered garments and shod you with badger skin; I wrapped you with fine linen and covered you with silk. I adorned you with ornaments, put bracelets on your hands, and a chain on your neck. I put a ring in your nose, earrings in your ears, and a crown of beauty on your head.

"Thus you were adorned with gold and silver, and your clothing was of fine linen, silk, and embroidered cloth. ... You were very, very beautiful, and advanced to royalty. Your name spread among the nations because of your beauty, for it was perfect through My magnificence which I had set on you," says the Lord Jehovah.

Ezekiel 16:8-14

For as many as have been baptized into Christ, you have put on Christ.
Galatians 3:27

What a vision of loveliness! He clothes His Bride with – Himself! "... that we might become God's righteousness in Him" [2 Corinthians 5:21]. She is truly a radiant Bride, shining with the Glory of God's own righteousness.

Again this is not so that she might present herself to Him, but that "*He might present to Himself the glorious Church without spot or wrinkle or anything like that, but that she might be holy and without blemish.*" Imagine His utter joy to find that indeed she becomes as beautiful as He knew she would be when He first saw her – us – in the gutter!

The Blushing Bride

Now the Bridegroom takes His Bride to His Table, to be seated in front of all the powers of the universe, the Court of Heaven, in the presence of the mighty angels – she who was once just a street urchin. Although she may blush (as she – we – well should) at being in the presence of such company, how pleasant it is to know that Jesus has no hesitation at having her sit next to Him. What a joy it is to bask in the warm glow of His Love that has brought her to this place.

And then He feeds His Bride – no, more than that, He gives Himself as totally as He can to her. He withholds nothing of Himself, not His life, not His being, not His Love, not His joy. After all, this is His Beloved Bride.

5. This is MY Child!

Adoption

Destined to be His Children

It is the Bridegroom Who has washed His Bride to spotless beauty. It is His wedding feast to which she comes. The Father-in-law has her sit with her Beloved on the throne in the heavenly places.

But that is not enough. The Bride is no mere satellite to the nuclear family of God. The Father takes a further extraordinary step. He adopts the Bride.

> He predetermined us for adoption to Himself through Jesus Christ, according to the good pleasure of His will, to the praise of the Glory of His grace in which He endowed us with grace in the Beloved, in Whom we have redemption through His Blood, the forgiveness of trespasses according to the riches of His grace which He *lavished* upon us …
> Ephesians 1:5-8

What exuberance! Not just the wedding, even the adoption was long planned and long awaited. The Father has been on the edge of His seat, waiting to pour out "lavishly" all the riches of His grace.

God's Child

> For you did not receive a spirit of slavery to again be afraid, but you have received a spirit of sonship, in which we cry, "Abba! Father!" – the Spirit Himself bears witness with our spirit that we are God's children, and if children, then heirs: indeed God's heirs and joint-heirs with Christ, provided we jointly suffer in order that we may also be jointly glorified.
> Romans 8:15-17

This is extraordinary! "Abba!" – "Dad," the child's version of "Ab" (Father) – is a term of familiarity and endearment[11]. We run to the arms of the Almighty God of the whole wide Universe, He Who is above every angel and power and principality, He Whose Word creates and cannot be thwarted, He Who judges the world in righteousness and holiness – we call HIM, "Dad"?? Yes!!

Even more astonishing, is that this is not us. It sounds like our voice when we pray – but St Paul insists: "the Spirit Himself bears witness with our spirit that we are God's children" – it is not just us, it is the Holy Spirit praying through us – by this He certifies that we really are God's Beloved children.

Joint-Heirs

What should really astound us are these words, "if children, then heirs: indeed God's heirs and joint-heirs with Christ." God will have no second-class children! The Bride is regarded by the Father as Beloved as the Son is. Everything that the Father pours out toward His Son – His extraordinary Love, His gifts – is given undiminished to the Bride. There is no favoritism. There are no leftovers.

Yet this also expresses a remarkable principle which has been designed into the creation of the world: "provided we jointly suffer with Him in order that we may also be jointly glorified." As we observe life in this world, it seems, at first, to be a puzzle in that God – with Whom all things are possible [Matthew 19:26] – appears to be "hampered": Where is He at work? After all, He has no physical form by which we can recognize Him and therefore by which to see Him in action. Yet this is by His deliberate choice!

Naturally the universe could have been created in such a way where He would be obviously seen (which happens already in heaven). But, rather, His plan is to make *humans* be the essential partner in what He does. What activity among mankind does God do that does not depend on humans? Whether it be telling people about His Good News, or touching the hurts of a person, or feeding the hungry, or whatever the task may be, humans are the *visible* means by which He accomplishes these things. If we refuse to do a certain task, then it simply will not get done. God will not use angels, He will not do it in any other way – thousands will die of starvation, thousands will never hear the Good News, if we decide not to do these essential tasks.

He is that serious about making the Bride vital to His Plan. She is to be no stay-at-home goddess-on-a-pedestal. She is to be where the Bridegroom is, considered by Him as unmistakably indispensable, working and suffering side-by-side with Him, sharing in His struggles and sharing in His glory.

My Child, My Beloved

> This is My Son, the Beloved, in Whom I am well pleased
> Matthew 3:17; 12:18; 17:5

Imagine any father saying, "This is my son!" – what a powerful sense of joy and pride those words declare! And now, in the adoption ceremony of Baptism, God proclaims before angel, devil, in fact, the whole universe:

> "Hey, everybody! This is MY son, MY daughter – MY Beloved – in whom I am well pleased!"

We are born anew:

> Blessed be the God and Father of our Lord Jesus Christ, Who according to His great mercy, having caused us to be born again into a living hope through Jesus Christ's resurrection from the dead, and to an inheritance imperishable, undefiled, and unfading, held fast in heaven for you,
> I Peter 1:3, 4

of imperishable seed:

> having been born again, not of perishable but of imperishable seed, through the abiding Word of the living God;   I Peter 1:23

wrapped in Christ

> For you, as many as were baptized into Christ, have put on Christ.
> Galatians 3:27

– imagine the Father's unquenchable delight!

Partakers of the Divine Nature

Partakers

> His divine power has given to us all things which pertain to life and godliness, through the knowledge of Him Who has called us to His own glory and virtue; through which He has given to us exceeding great and precious promises: that through these you might be partakers of the divine nature…   II Peter 1:3-4

"Partakers" – what a staggering thought! However this does not mean that we become little gods. "Partaker" [*koinonia* – participation/communion] is the origin of the word St Paul uses in I Corinthians 10:16:

> The Cup of Blessing which we bless, is it not a *participation* in Christ's Blood?
> The Bread which we break, is it not a *participation* in Christ's Body?

In this feast, Jesus the Bridegroom gives His very self to His Bride. It is *His Divine Nature* which enters us, becomes one with us: we live in Him, He lives in us – image upon image overflows with the lavishness of "the riches of His grace"! The enthusiasm, the delight, the Love from God is unstoppable.

"Stuck" With Us – No Back Door

The atmosphere of adoption is the atmosphere of Love – He *chooses* us [Ephesians 1:4; II Thessalonians 2:13]. It is a relationship designed and entered into by God, not because we insist, but because He insists: He commands it [Matthew 20:28]; He requires it [John 3:5]; it is His will [John 1:12-13]. No foster children for Him ever! He wants the Bride to unmistakably know for certain that she is indeed His.

When the New Testament was written, the civil law was such that a natural-born child might be disowned, but the adopted child can never be discarded. The inheritance can never be withdrawn. The adopting parent is "stuck" with the child.

Why does God select the word "adoption" to describe His relationship to us? It is His solemn guarantee He will never back out on us. Although the "natural-born" Son would be forsaken [Matthew 27:46], "never will I forsake you" [Hebrews 13:5]. He will never stop lavishing the riches of His grace upon the Bride.

We Can Reject – The Prodigal Son [Luke 15:11-24]

> the younger of them said to his father, 'Father, give me the share of property that falls to me.'   v 12

Although this son is not adopted, the father's powerful commitment is visible. In so many words, the son is saying, "Dad, drop dead. And if you will not oblige, at least give me the inheritance that I would get if you had." Now for many farmers, the land is more than a workplace, it is also their life – the farm is integral with their identity. All that they are, and often what they profit, gets "plowed" back into the land, to improve it, to make it grow, to make it better for the offspring that will follow.

This son wants all the benefits, while rejecting the father.[12] Imagine the extreme hardship that is placed upon a farm in attempting to liquidate the son's share! Cattle, machinery, even land may have to be sold. Workers may have to be let go. The workload and the debt suddenly become much heavier on the remaining family.

As well, it is evident that with this attitude, one just knows what the son will do with the generations-won inheritance once he gets his hands on it. It is no wonder that the older, more responsible son would have such strong resentment toward his brother.

"He went and was joined to one of the citizens of that country" [v 15] – ultimately when his lifestyle gives out, the younger son hands his life over to an outsider, and ends up in a pigsty. Although God cannot break *His* commitment to us, like that son, we too can reject our relationship with Him and "join with" someone/thing else – and also end up "in the pigsty."

"But while he was still far distant, his father saw him" [v 20] – the father has been searching the horizon every day, despite the son's rejection. Joy, eagerness, enthusiasm – Love – mark the father's response as soon as he recognizes his son: *he runs to him!* His forgiveness casts aside the son's earlier rejection in order to renew the relationship for which the Father still yearns.

We've Only Just Begun

As with any newborn child, the family relationship is filled with all kinds of potential. It is a potential that can be rejected, or lay dormant, or it can be developed every day. "Jointly suffer" with Him [Romans 8:17, above] carries the same idea as "to deny yourself, take up your cross daily and follow Me" [Luke 9:23] – it is to order one's life so as to reflect the new heritage one has. It is to live the death of sin and the newness of the resurrection. It is the distinctiveness of being God's person in a world that cannot understand such motivation, a world that does not like such a visible reminder of God's will. It is to be non-conformist in a sin-filled, selfish, rebellious world.

By Grace

The initiative comes from the Father. Paul reminds us: "while we were still sinners ... while we were enemies" [Romans 5:8, 10] is our state when the Bridegroom reaches out His hands and they are nailed to a cross. John declares that Jesus died for the sins "of the whole world" [I John 2:2] – all humanity. The Father invites *every* person to come to faith. It is by *Grace*.

Grace, as an example, is *not* like the misconception that our repentance causes God to forgive us, despite how in earnest we may be. Rather it is the other way around: God's forgiveness causes us to repent. By nature we are afraid to see our sin: if we should grasp what we are really like according to God's holiness and if there were no solution to which we could turn, our only result would be deep and utter despair. Such a prospect is too terrifying for us to risk and therefore we would never allow such an awareness to creep in if we could avoid it.

So God's forgiveness must come first. But once we are set into this safe and secure environment, now there is freedom, freedom to realize just how infected with sin we are and how deep it goes. The freedom lies within the knowledge that we can immediately be rid of the sins, as we *with joy* hand them over to God since we *already know* what He will do with them: "As far as the east is from the west, so far has He removed our rebellions from us" [Psalm 103:12]. We do not have to *plead with* and *convince* God to forgive, His forgiveness has to plead with and convince *us* to repent.

He has set the stage with His grace and mercy, which now calls forth faith on our part; so also His Adoption, Baptism, creates a safe and secure environment in which faith can grow – not because we have desired this relationship, but because He has initiated it and insists on it. The Father wants the Bride to know for certain that she is not just merely welcome but is eagerly sought out to be His child.

6. He Said So

Overwhelmed

Sometimes it can be overwhelming. There is just so much to be found in the Bridegroom's Feast! How often we have come to the altar and returned, and it is over so quickly. It is hard to comprehend that something of enormous consequence, something profound, has actually occurred. Often we do not feel / see / realize / think of / understand all the things which are supposed to be going on. We really ought to pay more attention to the significance of the moment, but often we are distracted by the procedures surrounding Communion and then it is already over.

The whole occasion is characterized by an almost seemingly routine air about it. Looking around the church, everything seems unchanged and merely commonplace. Should there not be a far more dramatic event when it comes to such a significant experience which has such powerful and long-term effects? Have we missed the value, and now it is gone?

What is Faith?

Technical Language

In answer, it would be useful to first pause to discuss "faith." How should "faith" be defined – especially without using the words "believe" or "trust"? Some think they must "spiritualize" the meaning because after all, we are talking about spiritual matters. So some may quote

> And faith is the substance of what is hoped for, the proof of things (Greek word: pragmatos – "pragmatic") not seen.   Hebrews 11:1

This is a good explanation, however it is *St Paul's* definition. How would *you* describe it?

When someone says to you "You should have more faith," what are you supposed to *do*? And if faith is the Holy Spirit's work, not of human origin, then how are we supposed make ourselves "have more faith"?

If we who are inside the Church have trouble with the language, imagine those outside who do not have a clue as to what we talk about! If we use a word that we ourselves cannot adequately define or even really understand, then it suggests that we have a far more technical language than we realize, along with only a fuzzy and weak grasp of its meaning as well.

Faith as Feeling

Do I have to feel something (for example, "heart strangely warmed" or "burning in the breast") in order to have faith?

Feelings are like icing to the cake – some cakes taste so good with their icing (there is nothing like when the heart and spirit soar in joy, when God feels so close that you could almost touch Him). But not every cake has icing. And some only have a powdering of icing sugar.

As in Love so also for faith, feelings are not reliable as a criteria. For instance, if a person had a particularly hard day, coming home, he pours himself into an easy chair – that "puddle" in the chair is him. His spouse, needing some affirmation, asks, "Honey, do you love me?" Likely he is not "feeling" love – only fatigue. Yet despite the lack of "feeling," it does not mean that he has ceased to love.

When God's great Love is described [John 3:16; Romans 5:8; Ephesians 2:4-7], the measure of His Love is not in what He feels, but in what He does. Our faith also must be described by its effect on our life.

> So also faith by itself, if it has no works, is dead. Someone will say, "You have faith and I have works. Show me your faith without the works, and I from my works will show you the faith." James 2:17-18

Because She Said So!

A woman calls her doctor for an appointment and the receptionist tells her, "Next week Wednesday, at 1 PM." After she hangs up, perhaps already she is making plans for transportation; her schedule may need to be altered, it may affect how she will dress for the day; she may want to take a bath and wash her hair; she may need to gather information and decide on questions to ask; she must go to a specific location and show up at the appointed time fully expecting the medical staff to be ready for her.

Based upon the receptionist's word, her life is altered to conform to the promise. It is merely a common reflex action; one does not stop to decide whether or not to believe the receptionist's word, or to convince oneself that this appointment will happen, or to concentrate on her words, or to do some sort of mental gymnastic which some seem to think needs to be done in order to "have faith." It is simply the automatic response to a promise – "because she said so." And note the bewilderment if the doctor's office is *not* ready for her!

Because *HE* Said So!

It is no different when the Bridegroom gives His Word. He does not make it flowery. He does not embellish it – He never has to add, "cross my heart, and hope to die." He has declared what He would do and what He will give, simply stated, and that is His Word on the matter.

Based upon, for example, a receptionist's word, we make adjustments to our lives frequently – would the Bride do any less when the Bridegroom gives her His Word? The bonus is that whereas sometimes human plans go awry, Jesus' plans never do. He will do, and will accomplish, and will give as He said He would.

His Word Depends on Him – Based on His Character

The Bridegroom gives His Word. That Word does not depend on whether we understand what or how, whether we grasp all of it, nor even if we are aware of all of it.

His Word depends on Himself, and therefore it happens. It does not even depend on whether we are ready to "receive" His promises. After all, we are the Bride whom He picked out of the gutter, whom He washed, whom He dressed, just so that He could present us to Himself without spot.

The Bride's main concern, therefore, is not to grasp everything her Beloved is doing, but rather to put herself totally into His hands, and He will accomplish the good things He has designed for her since from before the world was created.

His Trustworthiness - Supernatural For Us

Not In Our Nature

To be so convinced of the trustworthiness of God is not easy. In fact, it is not natural.

> in whom the god of this age has blinded the thoughts of the unbelievers, so that the illumination of the Gospel of the glory of Christ, Who is the image of God, does not shine out.   II Corinthians 4:4
>
> For the heart of this people has become sedentary, and they hear with fattened ears, and they have closed their eyes, lest they should perceive with the eyes, and hear with the ears, and understand with the heart, and turn back that I should heal them.   Matthew 13:15

Our sinful (i.e., rebellious) natures are too far into defiance to even want to consider trusting God. We do not want Him telling us what to do, or what to be, or anything. We do not expect that His heart would be interested in us. For us to suddenly depend on God, to trust Him, to worship Him, means something profound has had to happen down to our very natures.

The Rebellious Revolutionized

Since it is not in our nature, the confidence of taking Jesus at His Word comes only when our nature is overwhelmed by an outside source:

> Therefore I want you to understand that ... no one can say "Lord Jesus" if not by the Holy Spirit.   I Corinthians 12:3

Faith is not some human response to a divine promise, it is the active involvement of God Himself to turn the inclination of our natures around and create the faith required. *Now* things begin to happen – changes are made in our lives: perspectives are re-oriented and cleared up – now we begin to see God for what His heart really is about; attitudes are re-formed – now we look forward to what God's heart has in store for us; adjustments are begun throughout our lives – after all, He gave us His Word – "because He said so!"

The Power of His Word

Even When We are Unaware, His Word Still Works

Although she may not remember everything, or think of everything, or even feel anything at the moment of Holy Communion, the Bride can be assured that that does not thwart the Bridegroom. He has brought to bear all that He gave His Word on. All of it is present and active, whether seen or not seen, recognized or not.

> So shall My Word be that goes out of My mouth; it shall not return to Me empty, but it will do that which I please, and it shall prosper in that which I sent it. Isaiah 55:11

There will always be times when only in retrospect the Bride will discover what the Bridegroom has been doing all along. At such times there will be gratitude and praise of Him. And now she may make use of these gifts already given. Or not.

But that does not stop the Bridegroom from fulfilling His Word. And in the next Communion, all this will be accomplished yet once again. Again the Bridegroom will make good on His Word, even when the Bride does not know it, recognize it, or realize it.

The Implications of His Word

How does one know that he is Loved by God? How does one know that he has been forgiven? How does one know that God is with him? How does one know that He will work all things together for good? And what about all the other promises? How does one know? Simply because *He said so*. Sometimes it does not *seem* that way. Sometimes it does not *feel* that way. Sometimes it does not *look* that way.

But He gave His Word, backed by His Cross – *that* is what we depend on. When in Holy Communion the Bridegroom has so personally touched His Bride, it cannot be that His Word will not be accomplished in and to her – God is just too powerful for us to go away from His Table and not be different in some way – the touch of God cannot be without effect, the Word of God cannot be void [Isaiah 55:11] (even when we are determined to resist it, it will have effect, although it may be in the hardening of our hearts).

Did one miss the specialness of the moment at the instant of Communion? It makes no difference – God has still acted, and everything that occurs in those few seconds can be discovered, appreciated, built upon, and used every day following, because His Word is actually fulfilled – "because *HE said so*."

Sophisticated Faith?

Become Like a Child

... Jesus was incensed, and said to them, "Permit the children to come to Me, do not hinder them; for to this sort belongs God's Kingdom.

> Truly, I say to you, whoever does not welcome God's Kingdom like a child shall never enter it."   Mark 10:14-15

> Having called a child, He set him in the midst of them, and said, "Truly, I say to you, unless you turn about and become as the little children, you never will enter the Kingdom of Heaven – therefore whoever will humble himself like this child, he is the greatest in the Kingdom of Heaven."   Matthew 18:2-4

Child. Young child. It is used to refer to the age-two-or-under child Jesus in Matthew 2. Jesus takes up a young child into His arms in Mark 9:36. The kind of faith we have been talking about, such uncomplicated and life-influencing trust, is often so visible in a young child. We pay a lot of lip-service to becoming like a child – well, because Jesus says it is a good thing.

Must Be an Adult

But to get down to reality: children are not allowed when it comes to the important things of faith. They must reach "an age of reason," or "an age of accountability," or "an age of …" The less child-like, the more adult-like they are, well, do you not see how that is so much better?

So when it comes to the means/ways by which God gives His grace, has it subtly become a matter of achievement: achieving a level of knowledge, achieving a level of maturity, achieving some spiritual "experience," achieving some level of adult-measured commitment?

Despite that God's grace comes "not of works, lest anyone should boast" [Ephesians 2:9], must one *qualify* in order to receive grace? Perhaps "being like a child" only works if you are an adult trying to be like a child, rather than a child being a child.

Tension Between Faith and ...

The childlike faith holds on to the promises, even those concepts which it cannot fully grasp: how this Feast is based on God's Grace; how it springs from the depths of God's heart; how its effects come solely from the power of God's Word, how it is the very presence of Bridegroom for His Bride (*all of His Bride*). Truly, the more one knows about this Gift, the theory is that we will the more greatly value it and will use it. However, one must also realize sinful human nature also has its effects on how we will really regard such gifts of God, no matter what the age.

Yet just what is God doing anyway despite when we are ignorant or shallow in our understanding? If God's Word, power and work were limited by our grasp of them, how impoverished we would be.

Our knowledge, commitment, maturity do not motivate the Bridegroom Who has been motivated from His heart from before the world was created. Merely a simple, expectant faith is required – which is what we admit when we recognize that even the mentally challenged receive all of God's mercy, grace and promises – purely and only "because *He said so.*"

The Presence

Powerful Affirmation of His Word

> Yet if I were to speak according to the usage of Scripture, I should have only one single Sacrament, but with three sacramental signs...
> Martin Luther[13]

That single Sacrament Luther refers to is that the Bridegroom Himself comes in Person: that is what fills His Word with content; that is what gives

Baptism and Communion their power. Often we accent how the Sacraments bring "forgiveness of sin, life and salvation" – but do we miss the real point which Luther is making? Have we focused on the results without seeing the Presence?

Jesus says, "I am the Resurrection and the Life; … I am the Way, and the Truth, and the Life; …" [John 11:25; 14:6] – He does not say that He "has," He "brings," He "gives," but rather He "IS" the Resurrection, Life, Way, and Truth. These "things" are one and the same with His Person, they are identical to Him. We come to receive *Jesus*, and *that* is why we then simultaneously receive "Life" and "forgiveness" and all the rest.

Because He Said So

In regard to Holy Baptism, Luther wrote:

> How can water do such great things?
> Water does not make these things happen, of course. It is God's Word, which is with and in the water. Because, without God's Word, the water is plain water and not a baptism. But with God's Word it is a Baptism, a grace-filled water of life, a bath of new birth in the Holy Spirit … Martin Luther[14]

Scotch taping words to the Bread, or dissolving them in the Wine, or soaking them in water is useless. But John 1 identifies that God's "Word" is wrapped in the Person of Jesus – when that Word is present and involved, then Jesus is present and involved. With that Presence, now these Sacraments become exactly what they are described to be and God is working in them. Things happen because God's Word will not be feeble, God's presence will not be impotent, God's touch cannot have no effect.

7. Presenting the Bride

Company's Coming!

The Guest List

Would a caterer be impressed if it were casually mentioned to him that the guest list included maybe a few billion people? Actually, in this case, He would not. After all, He is also the Host.

This is really one of the special things about Holy Communion: it has the ancient Hebrew concept of "remembrance," where we do not merely repeat a commemoration ceremony as we would on Memorial Day, but rather are drawn back into a moment that has no time, drawn back to the very Table where Jesus first said, "This is My Body… This is My Blood…" We do not repeat that occasion; rather we are drawn into that first gathering on the night in which Jesus is betrayed.[15]

In various places, Paul speaks about the Body of Christ, the fullness of the concrete unity of all believers that spans all distance and spans all ages, the Body that is connected to its Head, Jesus. It is on All Saints' Day where we catch a fleeting glimpse of the awesome impact of this feast, for on this day we celebrate the great gathering of this Body at our Lord's festal Table.

We are reminded that where Christ is, there is the fullness of His Body. Just as our heads cannot be separated from our bodies, so Jesus cannot be separated from His believers. Every believer has been made part of the Body of Christ, as real as our fingers and toes and heart and lungs are part of our bodies. This Body intersects with eternity: there is no time, there is no location on earth, there are no denomination. If one is a member of the Body of Christ, then he is where Jesus is.

If only we could freeze the moment of Holy Communion and then take a moment to look around. On that side are John, James, Peter, Thomas, Mary and Martha; and here are Paul, Barnabas, Lydia, Priscilla and untold early Christian martyrs; over there are the great Church fathers Eusebius, Augustine and St Francis; also the reformers John Hus, Martin Luther, John Calvin; and then there are the Wesley brothers, the remarkable hymnwriter Fanny Crosby and the translator Catherine Winkworth; and literally a "multitude which no man can number" [Revelation 7:9]. It's amazing how many can fit at that little Table of the Lord's!

Look! There are also people from Russia and South America; some newly martyred from Africa, and some from the underground churches in China. Over there are some worshippers gathered in Palestine, some behind closed doors in Iran, faithful believers in Sweden and stalwart Christians in North Korea.

There's Grandma in her apron, and Uncle George. There's the son who died young, and the aunt who died old. There's the friend from whom the continent now separates us, and Sally from down the street.

There are even Christians not yet born.

They are all here. No one is missing. All have come and are at Table with the Lord – at Table with *us*.

Never Alone

This is the Bride of Christ which in Ephesians 5 He washed with water and the Word in Baptism: His Wife, the Holy Jerusalem of Revelation chapters 19 and 21. This sense of unity throughout the ages is indeed very wonderful, but it also has a very practical application. Martin Luther wrote that one of the necessary aspects of Holy Communion is a word that has only two letters difference from Communion, the concept of *community*:

> Here we not only need the help of the community [of saints] and of Christ, in order that they might with us fight this sin, but it is also necessary that Christ and his saints intercede for us before God. ... Therefore take heart and be bold! You are not fighting alone. Great help and support are all around you. Martin Luther[16]

Two or three believers, huddled behind locked doors, or in some concentration camp, are suddenly thrust into the midst of this great host. They are not alone.

Those who are addicted seeking to be free from this stranglehold on their life come to the Table, there to find many hands lifting them in prayer, many scarred by the same bonds. They are not alone.

The lonely, the downtrodden, the bewildered, the grieving, all find that they are welcome, all have a home. They are not alone.

A famous actress, who in later life received an important award, remarked afterwards that she was struck by melancholy because, "I have no one to share the good news with." But not so at *this* Table! There is a great shout of praise and joy when good things happen to each other. They are not alone.

We are not just this little group. We are not just this little church. We are not just this little denomination. We are the Bride of Jesus Christ, God's own Holy, chosen People. What we do here at this Table at the direction of the Christ Who is the Head of the Body takes place in the midst of a great throng of His People throughout the world and throughout history, as Jesus reaches out through us to all whom He has so powerfully Loved in this world.

A Wonderful and Comforting Connection

The Place of Connection

> We cannot divide the Body of Christ. The Church militant [on earth] and the Church triumphant [in heaven] form one Church. Nothing can separate the members of the Church, neither life nor death, nor power, nor principalities. At the Altar we have fellowship with our risen and ascended Lord. But there is also a fellowship with all the members of the Church. At the Altar we join hands not only with the great saints in Heaven, but also with all our Loved ones who have passed within the veil, our faithful departed...
>
> The Church tells her children that there is a communication possible; that there is a medium between our departed ones and ourselves, and only one – it is our Blessed Lord Himself... To countless Christians the reality of the Communion of Saints has been an unfailing source of love and joy in the face of otherwise heartbreaking bereavement....
>
> The living Christ creates and guarantees this joyful fact. It is Christ, and not just our wishful hoping, who assures us that nothing can pluck out of His hand those who loved Him and trusted Him.... It is found in these words, "Because I live, ye shall live also."...
>
> ...We must come to a sense of the continuing presence of our loved ones, and we can do this if we realize the presence of our Living Lord. As we seek and find our Risen Lord we shall find our dear departed. They are with Him, and we find the reality of their continued life through Him....

...How pathetic it is to see men and women going out to the cemetery, kneeling at the mound, placing little sprays of flowers and wiping their tears from their eyes, and knowing nothing else. How hopeless they look. Oh, that we could take them by the hand, away from the grave, out through the cemetery gate, in through the door of the church, and up the nave to the very Altar itself, and there put them in touch, not with the dead body of their loved one, but with the living soul who is with Christ at the Altar. Our human nature needs more than the assurance that some day and in some way we shall again meet our loved ones "in heaven."....

My loved one has just left me[17]... But I am in touch with her. I know that there is a place where we can meet. It is at the Altar. How it thrills me when I hear the words of the Liturgy, "Therefore with angels and archangels and all the company of Heaven," for I know that she is there with that company of Heaven, the Communion of Saints, with the Lord. The nearer I come to my Lord in Holy Communion, the nearer I come to the saints, to my own loved ones. I am a member of the Body of Christ, I am a living cell in that spiritual organism, partaking of the life of the other cells, and sharing in the Body of Christ Himself.

Bernard von Schenk[18]

"All the Company of Heaven"

Jesus declared to the Sadducees (who claimed "that there is no resurrection, nor angel, nor spirit" [Acts 23:8]) an essential reality:

> But concerning the resurrection of the dead, have you not read what was spoken to you by God, saying, 'I am the God of Abraham, and the God of Isaac, and the God of Jacob'? He is not the God of the dead, but of the living.   Matthew 22:31-32

Can we really say that the saints of old – or of recent time – are here as well? Yes, because God "is not the God of the dead, but of the living!" When one is in Christ, he LIVES! All who are in Christ LIVE.

> I am the Resurrection and the Life; he who believes in Me, even if he die, yet shall he live, and all who live and believe in Me shall never die.
>
> John 11:25-26

In Jesus, time and space collapse into the moment of eternity. We are in the midst of a great throng of His People throughout the world and throughout history because the Body of Christ (and that is *all of it*) is *here*, as He reaches out to us and all whom He has so powerfully Loved in this world.

A Working Reality

As this writer had opportunity to look over some of his deceased father's correspondence, this same understanding and confidence were also expressed. In one letter he wrote to a grieving widow:

> We shall be thinking of you and Dick when we come to the Lord's Table, when our Father gathers us to receive His special food for His children. Here we are gathered before the Lord Jesus at the Altar. The Revelation tells us that our Lord, the Lamb of God, is seated on the Throne behind the Great Altar, in front of it is the Church; the countless numbers of saints. So we come to join in the worship of the Church in the Communion; we are one in Christ, whether here or there. Here we join in singing the great praise songs – and if we listen closely we can hear Dick's voice. O, what a blessing in the Sacrament, as the Lord feeds us with the Heavenly Food we seek and need to sustain us in this life.

And to a seminarian:

> God bless you both. Since you have been receiving the Blessed Sacrament regularly, I am happy to know that we have been walking together with the Lord along His Way of Sorrows. This Sunday we shall meet you in the Procession with the Palms, and gather at the Empty Tomb the next. It is a wonderful experience to know these eternal

truths in [such a] personal and intimate way through the Sacrament. A most Blessed Easter to you both.

This is no mere doctrine – it is a reality that surrounds us, that allows us to rejoice in the presence of His People, no matter if the congregation be large or small, no matter if physically present or present "in Christ."

All Around You

Impressed? We should be. It is indeed amazing to discover how many have joined us in this simple yet significant meal! This is one of the most extraordinary things about Holy Communion: ALL have come, from all places, from all time, giants of faith, and those who barely squeak in. No one is missing, none slip through the cracks, none are overlooked, – AND – WE have come.

The Bridegroom is at the Table. The Bride is at the Table. All is ready, for all in Christ have come.

The Body of Christ

An Extraordinary Expression

One of St Paul's most powerful word images is that of the Body of Christ:

> "Body of Christ" is an extraordinary expression. It is without parallel even in the Old Testament. Seneca, to be sure, was quite ready to refer to the citizens of Rome as a body politic. We are quite familiar with terms "student body" or "church body." To speak of church members as a body of Christians creates no particular excitement. However, that is not what the apostle chose to write. He spoke of Christians as the "body of Christ." That is to say, in some mysterious sense the church is

an extension of the incarnation of our Lord. It does His work. It is His instrument within history to carry on Christ's mission of gathering all things under His lordship. Dr Martin H Scharlemann[19]

For just as the [human] body is one and has many members, and all the members of the body, being many, are one body, so also is Christ.
I Corinthians 12:12

Paul does not say, "so it is with Christ and the Church," or "Christ and believers," but rather, simply, "Christ." To Paul, apparently, "Christ" does not refer to just Jesus, but also includes His entire Body – all believers – Head and Body always as a seamless whole.

Fingers and Toes, Knees and Nose… – Individuals in the Body

In I Corinthians 12, what is so extraordinary about Paul's vision of the Body of Christ, first of all, is its concrete reality to him, but also that the differences in the People of God are by deliberate design (also Romans 12:4-8), differences as diverse as the hand, eye, ear, heart, tongue, and all the other parts of the human body.

How does the human body work? Each part is unique, having a special job that the rest of the Body cannot do. The grasp of the hand cannot be duplicated anywhere else on the Body. The ability to hear, to speak, to see, to taste, to pump the Blood, to bring a breath of fresh air into the Body, to run, to… are all abilities unique to distinctive parts of the body. What value and importance God has placed upon each individual member of the body! That in itself provides strong encouragement to each individual.

Whose Body?

But the Bride is Christ's Body, therefore when each part does the unique job given to it, it is expressing Christ Himself's presence and activity – *each* is Jesus' living proof that He is in the midst of His People! Hear the voice of the Beloved through him who is Christ's tongue; discern God's activity through the insight of her who is Christ's eyes; experience God's steadfast Love especially through him who is Christ's heart; lean on the quiet strength and encouragement through her who is the "bones" of Jesus.

God intended that no one, other than Jesus, would do "all things well" and we cannot be everywhere, doing everything at the same time. He compels us to need each other, to value each other, to depend on each other, to learn from each other, and to grow with each other.

But Certainly Not With Them!

Human nature immediately steps in. We would like to homogenize Christ's Body into one big indistinguishable, shapeless lump, usually based on where our own interests and abilities lie. After all, if we can do something well, then everybody else should, because … it is … easy (for us). If one cannot, then he is not trying hard enough. Or maybe she is defective.

> If the whole body were an eye, where is the hearing? If the whole body were hearing, where is the sense of smell?   I Corinthians 12:17

He does not see what we see?! He obviously does not belong with us … If there is something we cannot do well (although someone else can) – well, who needed it (or them) anyway. Or jealousy: what makes him think he is so good?! Or inferiority: I will never be a Billy Graham.

> If the foot should say, "Because I am not a hand, I am not part of the body," never for this reason would it not be a part of the body. And if the ear should say, "Because I am not an eye, I am not of the body," never for this reason would it not be a part of the body.
>
> I Corinthians 12:15-16

Noting the divisiveness and exclusiveness that too often marks the Church, how has the Bride ever survived from the first generation??

The Goal of the Diversity

Despite where one part of the Body just may not understand what, how, and perhaps even why another part does what it does, when the Church comes to grips with the reality that the differences are by *God's* design, then something wonderful can happen. Instead of one isolated single-task society, there is the appreciation of what others can bring into the work of the Church, and a seeking of those who have the gifts which a distinct group of the Body of Christ is lacking.

Such variety can be recognized and encouraged, knowing that God deliberately created this diversity. A rebuke (but not rejection) at times may be valid, as when a person (or denomination) wanders away from the Lord's stated will – but there will be humble caution in rebuking those who are merely different from oneself.

Rarely Realized

Unfortunately, it often may take some sort of tragedy to finally make the Church / congregation pull together the way Paul describes. Then, at least for the moment, the different abilities and gifts surface, and the Body of Christ lives and acts according to God's blueprint.

Unfortunately, when the crisis is over, God's People too often go back to business as was usual.

However, suppose a Church grabs hold of this concept of the unity in diversity, and the attitude is developed that every individual (even perhaps denomination?) is to be treasured for his (/its) unique combination of gifts/abilities – what a wonderful vision of God at work this presents. If the Bridegroom is truly unleashed through the many gifts and talents of His Bride, what amazing and powerful things would He do? In fact, some congregations seem to experience such a presence of the Lord in their midst. Then St Paul is discovered as really knowing what he is talking about when he says, "when each part is working properly, [this] makes bodily growth and upbuilds itself in Love" [Ephesians 4:16].

A "Nasty" Doctrine

But I Don't Like Him/Her

Holy Communion takes a decidedly nasty turn against us. It does not soothe our fears, and lull us back to sleep. Suddenly we are shoulder-to-shoulder eating the same Bread/Body and drinking from the same Cup/Blood with that person we thought is a little off the edge; or with that person with whom we do *not* feel comfortable (who does not do things the way that *we* do); or with that person of whom we are jealous – we are forced to participate together, to be partners with each other. More than that, here is that person who did us wrong – and *he is taking Communion ahead of us*!! Now what shall we do??? What's this person in ratty jeans doing next to us?

These are the people we have to respect? we have to learn from? we have to include? we have to grow with? Can't we just take remote Communion?[20]

No Little Worlds Unto Ourselves

It sure makes sense to have Communion less often!! And it's much better in the pews where you can safely choose with whom you will surround yourself. After all, when you come forward to the altar: one, you never know next to whom you might find yourself; and two, we now must stand *together* before God's unblinking eye.

Holy Communion confronts us with the ways we separate and stratify people in the Church. Through our conscience and in other ways, God exposes not spiritual barriers but rather the ones of sin which we have created between us and other individuals. We shrink from others because, after all, the person next to us may have germs, or at least, "cooties."

When St Paul talks about "Christ" in the firm conviction that Jesus and His Body are an inseparable unity, we find ourselves *already "in Communion"* with all sorts of people – and many are just not *our* sorts of people.

"Shaking Things Up a Bit"

Holy Communion is sort of like Jesus saying, "Let's see what happens when I shake things up a bit." He forces us together, forcing us to think and care about each other (especially if it is "common cup" because then we *really* have to care about others and their wellbeing). His message is: either deal with these things that separate His Church now, and therefore reap the blessings and benefits and joy that He has for us; or do it finally before His

Great White Throne, having cheated ourselves of all with which He could have blessed us.

Sadly, when we are done with Communion, we often seem to breathe a spiritual sigh of relief that nothing dramatic has happened today, and therefore we can return to life as it has always been. Jesus' response is sadly, "Well, OK ... but there will be a next time!"

At the Pleasure of the Bridegroom

Holy Communion never asks us whether we feel comfortable about all this. It never is intended to. It is intended to be the reality of the atmosphere of Connection that surrounds us. It is intended to be the reality of the atmosphere of God's Love that surrounds us. It is intended to be the joy and pleasure of the *Bridegroom* with His Bride – *all of His Bride*. It is intended to be the grand Feast of salvation that extends into eternity, but is tasted here on this earth. It is intended to be the Body of Christ practicing Who they are.

No Frankenstein Here

Patch Job?

A familiar movie story of Frankenstein describes how the good doctor patched together a body and made a monster ("It's alive! It's alive") who was at best clumsy, inarticulate, and very out of place in this world. Although he had all the parts, the connection between his head (brain) and the rest of him was not very good, and the life that he had was at best artificial.

Hmm. Sounds just like ... nah! couldn't be ... but ... sometimes ...

Yes, unfortunately that can too easily describe the Body of Christ as well. Although the Head sits on top of the shoulders, we really are not too sure just who is in charge. It seems as though there is a lot of background noise going on which competes for leadership.

The Headship of Jesus

A few years ago, St Paul's Episcopal Church[21] in Darien, Connecticut, under their rector, Father Everett Fullam, pursued a very fascinating concept concerning the headship of Jesus: if Jesus were the Head of that congregation, and if they (particularly the council) sought His will, then how could there be a split vote on what they were contemplating? Obviously some, perhaps all, were not listening, because Jesus would never be of a divided mind [Matthew 12:25]

They resolved that from that point on, they would never do anything without a unanimous agreement. One time the council had agreed to go ahead on something – except for one man. It was not as if he was against it or would not let them go ahead. It was just, well, something felt uncomfortable, but he could not tell them what. They immediately decided to give the matter another month of prayer and consideration. At the next meeting, *nobody* voted in favor of the matter.

The Still Small Voice

They were listening. They were listening to what sometimes is a still small voice [I Kings 19:11-13] sometimes from the most unlikely of sources – remember God once used the mouth of a jackass [Numbers 22:28-30],[22] and even the mouth of an enemy of the faith (for example, the High Priest [John 11:48-52]).

The council was listening with a humility that came from submitting to the will of the Bridegroom, their Head. That kind of commitment should defuse a lot of the powerplays and other shenanigans that so often go on in the church. Either you end up basically doing nothing of real meaning, or you end up listening to the Head.

Of course, there is no magic formula. There will even be times when nobody will listen. However, such a commitment to really seek the Lord's will rather than have Him merely rubber-stamp our majority decisions would seem to encourage caution rather than for some individual or a clique to plunge ahead with its own agenda.

Non-Artificial Life

It is doubtful the "villagers" (outsiders) will stop throwing stones at this "monster," but at least now that the Head is properly in charge of the Body, it should not be as clumsy.

Now rather than just trying to merely exist in the Body, the saints – Christians – become equipped

> into the work of ministry; into building up Christ's Body, until we all arrive at the unity of the faith and of the knowledge of God's Son; into a "finished" Man; into the measure of the stature of Christ's fullness.
> Ephesians 4:12-13

"Christ's fullness" – what a thought that is! Unity, knowledge, maturity – what a delightful picture of the Bride! One can actually catch glimpses of Jesus in the midst of His People. The joy of His heart, the abundance of His

Life, the reality of His presence is evident. Stronger in heart, stronger in hand, stronger in word, stronger in foot – and sometimes stronger in stomach – the saints are in ministry, each with the task given by the Head, all contributing to upbuild the Body.

Gifted

> There are varieties of gifts, but the same Spirit; there are varieties of ministries, but the same Lord; there are varieties of activities, but the same God Who works mightily in all things in every one. To each is given the Spirit's manifestation for the common good.
> I Corinthians 12:4-7

What makes every one of us who and what we are does not happen to fall together by chance. Even supposing that were so, in Baptism the Head would have the chance to design us yet again as He makes us "born anew." He has gifted each of us with special work/abilities as part of His Body. He has gifted each church with special work/abilities as a larger part of His Body. He has gifted each denomination with special work/abilities as part of His world-wide Body.

He never expected us to be perfect, yet He calls us to do the tasks He has set before His Bride. Jehovah is at work in the midst of ALL His People.

No Vestigial Parts

At the turn of the 19th century, the medical world listed over 180 parts of the body as "vestigial" – that is, useless items that were "leftovers" from wrong turns in evolution. We now know that there is *nothing* that is useless in the body, apparently not even the appendix.

It is no different with Christ's Body: tiny churches, which some might think should have been closed up long ago, can yet be virtual spiritual powerhouses of prayer, equipping the Christians in that locale or in other places for their work of ministry. Next year their doors may be closed, yet they will leave their mark in the Body of Christ, because their preoccupation is not on their survival, but rather on those tasks their Head, the Lord, has given them. That their doors are not closed means there are tasks yet to be done. In regard to both churches and individuals, the thought of each part of the Body must be "how can I serve my Lord with the task He has given me," not on "how do I compare against…" or "how can I survive…"

Life Both Ways

Holy Communion now becomes more than merely a one-way sharing of the Bridegroom with His Beloved Bride, now the Bride is also sharing herself without reservation. She gives herself delightedly, whole-heartedly, eagerly to her Beloved, and she discovers through the Lord the wonderful sharing that can go on within the Body of Christ. Not only do we see the heart of God, but now we see the heart of the Bride. This is truly Life!

Participation

Pick Me! Pick ME!

> The Cup of Blessing which we bless, is it not a participation in Christ's Blood?
> The Bread which we break, is it not a participation in Christ's Body?
> I Corinthians 10:16

Two are decided to be the captains of the teams. They look over the group in front of them. Alternately they choose from the diminishing group someone to be on their respective teams. One fellow waits and waits. Finally the last captain has no choice but to pick him, because there is no one else left. Obviously.

Thank God, this is not a team. We are not going to be that last guy, reluctantly chosen. The issue will never be: "What could God ever do with me?" That is because God does not chance to happen upon us. He has designed us.

koinonia

The word that St Paul uses for "participation" is a word made special by the Christian community: *koinonia* "fellowship". It has the meaning of full partnership within the life of the community.

> The first [brotherhood] is the divine, the heavenly, the noblest, which surpasses all others, as gold surpasses copper or lead – this being the fellowship of all saints. ... In this we are all brothers and sisters, so closely united that a closer relationship cannot be conceived. For here we have one baptism, one Christ, one sacrament, one food, one gospel, one faith, one Spirit, one spiritual body, and each person is a member of the other. No other brotherhood is so close ... Martin Luther[23]

This is not unity by association, it is unity by participation; this is not participation as in merely cooperative action, it is participation as in being grafted into the life-stream of God's involvement in this world, in His People. It is the awesome privilege of being allowed to share in God's activity in this world.

The Three Sides of *koinonia*

This *koinonia* encompasses: the state of fellowship; what one receives from the fellowship; and what one gives into the fellowship.

> Here your heart must go out in love and learn that this is a sacrament of love. As love and support are given to you, you in turn render love and support to Christ in His needy ones. ... There are those, indeed, who would gladly share the profits but not the costs. That is, they like to hear that in this sacrament the help, fellowship, support of all the saints are promised and given to them. But they are unwilling in their turn to belong also to this fellowship. They will not help the poor, put up with sinners, care for the sorrowing, suffer with the suffering, intercede for others, defend the truth, and at risk of [their own] life, property, and honor seek the betterment of the Church and of all Christians. ... They are self-seeking persons, whom this sacrament does not benefit.
>
> Martin Luther[24]

"My faith is between me and God and no one else" is a statement not possible in Holy Communion!

"All Men Will Know"

> In this all will know that you are disciples of Me, if you have Love among one another.   John 13:35

It is not merely just going to the altar, then coming back, and we are done with our participation. Nor is it simply rejoicing and glorying in the benefits that we receive. We are looked for, anticipated; there is a slot with our name on it, a place of honor within the activity of the Body, something that just fits us like a glove.

We are created to have worth and value; Jesus has made us to be necessary. If we look to the Body of Christ to help us, then we must also realize that we are the Body of Christ to someone else. They seek the face and heart of Christ in us. Again Peter's words:

> His divine power has given to us all things which pertain to life and godliness, ... that through these you might be participants (*koinonia*) of the divine nature... II Peter 1:3-4

God's nature comes into us, dwells in us, works through us – is visible in us.

"As I Have Loved You"

> A new commandment I give to you, that you Love one another; as I have Loved you, so also you should Love one another. John 13:34

> Now this is the fruit, that even as we have eaten and drunk the body and blood of Christ the Lord, we in turn permit ourselves to be eaten and drunk, and say the same words to our neighbor, Take, eat and drink; and this by no means in jest, but in all seriousness, meaning to offer yourself with all your life, even as Christ did with all that he had, in the sacramental words. Martin Luther[25]

> Hope does not humiliate us, because God's Love has been poured into our hearts through the Holy Spirit Who has been given to us.
> Romans 5:5

God's Life now courses through our veins – it is an intimacy beyond description. Christ makes us His Body, and firmly connects Himself to us. Thus we participate (*koinonia*) in the Divine Nature. Just as "when we cry, 'Abba! Father!' it is God's Spirit bearing witness with our spirit" (Romans 8:15-16), we have the reassurance that whatever we do in His will is nothing less than the hand of God through us. Our participation is so honored by God.

8. The Bride *He Loves*

Deniers, Betrayers, Cowards

St Peter

Clumsy Faith

Peter often means well, but frequently gets himself into trouble: he walks on water, but then sinks [Matthew 14:28-32]; he confesses Jesus as the Christ, then has to be rebuked [Matthew 16:16-23].

Accommodating Faith

In Galatians 2:11-21, St Paul tells of how Peter had tried to blend in, but instead made the Gospel confusing: After Pentecost, working in Antioch, he moved easily among the non-Jews (Gentiles). When a delegation from Jerusalem arrived, he became afraid of what they would think, so he separated himself from the non-Jews. The Antioch Church became bewildered, so Paul had confronted him in regard to the freedom of the Gospel – that God's salvation is totally by grace.

Denial

These same problems are just as serious while Jesus is on trial for His life: Despite Jesus' warning that this would happen and despite Peter's earlier bravado that he would never fail Jesus [Matthew 26:33-35], with oaths, cursing, swearing he denies ever knowing His Lord [Matthew 26:74, Mark 14:71].

Significance

This is more significant than it may first appear: In the early Church, during persecution, some denied the faith under threat of suffering and death. The Church struggled with whether these deniers, when they repented, were still welcome to be part of its fellowship – part of its Communion. But ultimately they did not exclude those who returned, despite the feeling that they had deserted their Lord under such conditions.

Even though Jesus already has known and has forewarned Peter, He does not hesitate in including Peter now at the Last Supper, as He washes Peter's feet [John 13:1-10; 21], and later at all future communions. In fact John 21, perhaps in answer to the Church's struggle, is the account where Jesus makes Peter specifically aware as to how he is indeed forgiven and reinstated in Jesus' confidence.

Those He Counted On When He Needed Support

Sleeping on the Job

> He came and found them sleeping; and He said to Simon Peter, "Are you asleep? Could you not pay attention for one hour?" ... And again He returned, He found them sleeping ... He came the third time and said to them, "Sleep on now and take your rest. It is enough! The hour has come; look, the Son of Man is handed over to the hands of sinners."
>
> Mark 14:37, 40, 41

Jesus is in extreme distress. How good it would be to have even moral support from those with whom He is closest. Yet as He pours out His heart, they fall asleep. How utter the loneliness must have felt for our Savior.

"deserted Him and fled" [Matthew 26:56] – even the *"Beloved" disciple!*

> Look, the hour ... has come, in which you will be scattered, each one to his own place, and you will leave Me alone. Yet I am not alone because the Father is with Me. These things I have spoken to you, so that in Me you may have peace. ... John 16:32-33

Along with Peter and the other disciples, even the "beloved" disciple flees as Jesus is captured, despite His forewarning and the bravado that all have claimed. Again when the Lord could have used the moral support, He is left standing alone.

Just Didn't "Get It"

> Peter answered him, "Explain this parable to us."
> He said, "Are you also still without understanding?" Matthew 15:15-16

After being with Jesus for years, it seems they still just do not have a clue in regard to what He is telling them. Then as they sit in misery the Saturday after the crucifixion, plainly they still do not understand nor even yet believe all that Jesus has revealed about His essential mission. Easter will be a total surprise to them all.

> O foolish ones – how slow of heart to believe all that the prophets spoke! Was it not necessary that the Christ suffer these things and enter into His Glory? Luke 24:25-26

Judas Iscariot – Perhaps A Participant?

Denier, Betrayer – How Much of a Difference?

Judas is warned by Jesus [Matthew 26:47, John 13:26] – so Peter also is warned. Judas sells out for money [Matthew 26:14-5] – Peter sells out for fear. Even at His capture, Jesus still reaches out to Judas [Luke 22:48], as He also later does with Peter [Luke 22:61]. Peter's response is to weep bitterly when he realizes what he has done [Matthew 26:75, Luke 22:62].

Judas seems not so much to have originally acted in malice toward Jesus. Rather, as Eve had "good intentions" [Genesis 3:6], so also he has "good intentions" (with a bit of entrepreneurial icing on top), perhaps to make Jesus finally "proclaim Himself" and assert His Messianic Kingship. When things do not turn out as anticipated (as happened to Eve and Adam), the fact that he is so troubled would demonstrate that he does really care about his Master. However without accepting Who Jesus is as Savior, and, being abandoned by those whose duty is to pronounce forgiveness (the priests [Matthew 27:4]), his response is suicide [Matthew 27:1-5].

Jesus has *always* known about Judas [John 6:64; 13:10-11, 21]. What is curious is that every time in his Gospel when John mentions Judas Iscariot, he emphasizes that this is the betrayer [6:71; 12:4; 13:2, 26; 18:2-5] – even more times than Matthew does. Since most commentators believe that the "Beloved disciple" [13:23; 19:26; 20:2; 21:7, 20] is John himself, could Judas be this Gospel writer's challenge? Because he is especially close to Jesus and the betrayal would have especially pierced his heart, perhaps the "Apostle of Love (*agape*)" struggles with his opinion about Judas as he writes his account of Jesus.

The Sop

Sometimes, much is made of "the sop" (John 13:26):

> Jesus answered, "It is he to whom I shall dip the morsel and give it." Having dipped the morsel, He gave it to Judas, Simon Iscariot.

Within the Passover tradition, "the sop" is normally given to a beloved person:

> In remembrance of the holy Temple, we do as the rabbis did in Temple times: He put matzah and bitter herbs together and ate them as a sandwich, in order to observe literally the words of the Torah: "They shall eat it [the Passover offering] with matzah and bitter herbs." *(Exodus 12:8 & Numbers 9:11)* ...
>
> This sandwich was eaten with Lamb during temples times in Jerusalem, it is also known as the sop. It is still the custom today to give this dipped sop with affection to a loved one.   David Sargent[26]

This would provide an interesting counterpoint to Judas' use of a symbol of being "beloved" – a kiss – and Jesus' use of "the sop" as a symbol of being "beloved." If indeed it is "the sop," then Jesus is not even now turning away from Judas, but rather, just as He does at the betrayal, reaches out His hand in Love to this confused sheep.

The difficulty is that we do not have a Hebrew term in the texts, only a Greek word which simply means "morsel."[27] Another difficulty is that Jesus dies on "the Day of Preparation" [Matthew 27:62; Mark 15:42; Luke 23:54; John 19:14,31] when the Passover lambs are being killed in anticipation of roasting them for the Passover *Seder* meal later. The Lord's Supper occurs the evening before[28], so is the dinner a true *Seder* celebration, since no lamb has been "officially" killed yet? If not, then the context for "the sop" might be entirely different. Further to muddy the waters is that Matthew 26:23

(who is writing to the Jews who would know the tradition) and Mark 14:20 speak of both Jesus and Judas dipping "the morsel" at the same time, although that does not preclude Jesus also giving "the sop" to Judas.

It is also true that Jesus does not always stand on tradition when something more important is involved, so that the Passover *Seder* meal cannot simply be dismissed as out of hand, although it may confuse the disciples as to why Jesus would eat it on this day.

So is Judas at the Sacrament?

There is a bit of confusion about John's account of Judas in the Last Supper. The translations that follow the King James Version have the Supper being ended in 13:2, which then suggests that the foot-washing and the announcement of Judas' betrayal occur afterwards. Luke [22:17-23] also suggests that the announcement of the betrayer occurs after the Sacrament.

On the other hand, the Greek word in John 13:2 could validly indicate that the Supper is still in process, not finished, which is the way many translations put it (for example, the Revised Standard Version).

If it is "the sop" that Jesus gives to Judas and this is the Passover *Seder* meal, since this part of the ceremony occurs prior to the breaking of the middle *matzah* called the *Afikomen* and the drinking of "the Cup of Salvation," then indeed Judas would seem to be gone from the table before Jesus institutes Holy Communion.

Although the probability is that Judas is not a communicant, there is a nagging reasonable possibility that He just may have been included. That small margin of doubt poses an intriguing question: having known from the beginning who will betray Him, why would Jesus still allow this holy Meal to someone *we* regard as so inappropriate? On what basis would Jesus permit him? This question could challenge us to rethink some of our automatic exclusions, and it may also call us to understand more about the Bridegroom's motivations – and therefore about what *we* should do in our stewardship to His will.

Defective Disciples – Some Grossly Defective

They do not understand. They do not even believe correctly. They are not "pure." They are not sinless. One disciple will deny any connection with Jesus. One disciple will reject Jesus' purpose for coming. Yet simply because of *their* love *for Him*, they all have come to that Supper – and Jesus *Loves them*.

> Before the feast of the Passover, Jesus knowing that His hour had come when He would depart out of this world to the Father, having Loved His own who were in the world, He Loved them to the end.   John 13:1

Jesus does not hesitate, but rather *earnestly desires* to have this meal with them [Luke 22:15], even at this point of time in their spiritual lives.

Who Approves the Bride?

The Feast of Communion is God's Idea

> For here we conclude and say: Even though a knave takes or distributes the Sacrament, he receives the true Sacrament, that is, the true body and blood of Christ, just as truly as when one [receives or] administers it in the most worthy manner. For it is not founded upon the holiness of men, but upon the Word of God. And as no saint upon earth, yea, no angel in heaven, can make bread and wine to be the body and blood of Christ, so also can no one change or alter it, even though it be misused.

> For the Word by which it became a Sacrament and was instituted does not become false because of the person or his unbelief. For He does not say: If you believe or are worthy, you receive My body and blood, but: Take, eat and drink; this is My body and blood. Likewise: Do this (namely, what I now do, institute, give, and bid you take). That is as much as to say, No matter whether you are worthy or unworthy, you have here His body and blood by virtue of these words which are added to the bread and wine.
>
> Martin Luther[29]

The wellspring of Communion lies not with man but with God. The festive Bridal Table is not given as merely another law or another dogma or another obligation or another ritual. This is God personally and intimately sharing Himself and He eagerly does it whether we receive it or not. Can it benefit us even when we misunderstand or lack in our understanding? YES! Because this is *His* gift; it is *His* heart made visible; it is *His* desire; it is His Word; it is *His* power at work. The pivot of the gift is not on the disciple but on JESUS.

Does Jesus Trust His Own Power?

> For the Word of God is powerful enough, when uttered, to change even a godless heart, which is no less unresponsive and helpless than any infant. So through the prayer of the believing church which presents it, a prayer to which all things are possible [Mark 9:23], the infant is changed, cleansed, and renewed by inpoured faith. *Nor should I doubt that even a godless adult could be changed, in any of the sacraments, if the same church prayed for and presented him, as read of the paralytic in the Gospel, who was healed through the faith of others [Mark 2:3-12].* I should be ready to admit that in this sense the sacraments of the New Law are efficacious in conferring grace, not only to those who do not, but even to those who do most obstinately present an obstacle. What obstacle cannot be removed by the faith of the church and the prayer of faith?
>
> Martin Luther[30] (Emphasis mine)

How powerful is Holy Communion? Is it as powerful as the other "Means of Grace," i.e., the Word and Baptism? The Holy Spirit using the Word of God can convert a soul. We agree with Luther as he maintains in this quote that through the prayer of the Church, when God's Word is attached to the waters of Baptism, the Holy Spirit creates faith in a resistant heart, such as in an infant's heart. But Luther appears to suggest that when God's Word is attached to the Bread and Wine, Holy Communion is the equal to Baptism, in which the Holy Spirit can also work faith in a rebellious heart – or is this Sacrament somehow only of lesser power?

It is here where the possible presence of Judas at the Last Supper raises the question: Does the Lord simply dismiss Judas as lost, or is He, even in this Sacrament, reaching into Judas' heart, to call forth faith in him? Is He even in this Holy Meal calling Judas to repentance, just as He does later at the betrayal [Luke 22:48]? Just what is Jesus' earnest desire, what is He most concerned about in His Supper, perhaps in contrast to *our* sensibilities? What precedent might He be establishing? What is at stake, if or when we admit that even a Judas is permitted at that first Lord's Supper?

Just how powerful is Holy Communion when it comes to God's work of salvation?

Welcomed by Jesus at His Table

> A Christian is holy in body and soul, whether he be layman or priest, man or woman. If anybody denies that, he speaks blasphemy against holy baptism, the blood of Christ, and the grace of the Holy Spirit. A Christian is a rare and wonderful thing, and God is more concerned about him than about the sacrament. For the Christian was not made for the sacrament, but the sacrament was instituted for the Christian.
>
> Martin Luther[31]

We do not know what a person will be like in the future but Jesus does! He accepts Peter – and perhaps even Judas – at His Table. His focus is not on "protecting" Himself, nor on "protecting" the Sacrament, but to "eagerly" share Himself in a profound way. What then does HE consider is essential for those who make up the Bride He Loves and feeds? How does one determine if someone is "Christian" enough?

What Marks a Participant in the Bride?

The Basic Requirements

The questions posed above are important and do need to be considered, but likely we will never be able to answer them adequately. The heart of another will always be a mystery to us. Should we therefore err on the side of caution and thereby exclude those whom Jesus Loves, whom *He* has invited to His feast? Yet might erring in the opposite direction lead to abuse and the trivializing of something that is far too precious?

The Church has struggled often and still does with identifying how to recognize those who are part of the Bride. However, it has established some useful benchmarks called the "creeds," which are a series of statements identifying crucial elements of doctrine, and a person who agrees to them in faith is considered a follower indeed of the Bridegroom.

The most simple creed – in use for almost 2000 years – is called "the Apostles' Creed" or "the Teaching Creed," and the Church has not really improved upon such a fundamental definition of Christian faith.

Yet even the creeds are built upon a more basic foundation: A believer must be one who acknowledges that he is a sinner (that is, a rebel against

God [I John 3:4]) who deserves God's judgment of death and repents of his sin; who believes that Jesus (truly God and truly man) has fully paid that penalty in his place; who desires deeply that God in all His three Persons be part of his life (even when all this is not understood very well, nor followed perfectly); and who has been Baptized, so that he has entered into the community of the faithful that spans time and eternity, that is, the Bride.

It is Not That Jesus is Obliged

How hard all this is, though! To believe properly does not give a person a "right" to commune, nor does it somehow compel or oblige Jesus to give of Himself to this person. Jesus shares Himself with the Bride He Loves because it is *His earnest delight* – it is something that erupts from *His heart*.

He does not stand officiously with clipboard in hand and pencil at the ready, checking a list to see whether every doctrine is adequately believed. Again Peter (and Judas?) drift into our view – in fact, all the disciples do, who at the Last Supper still lack understanding of their Lord's purpose on earth, and who certainly could not even imagine His death and especially His resurrection. Yet Jesus still eagerly gives of Himself to them. Just as significantly, none of us has perfect faith or knowledge – what then is adequate?

We cannot assume that defective understanding will prevent someone from receiving what is contained in this sacred Meal, because these are not "items" which are received, rather it is the *Person* of Jesus which is received. And in Isaiah 55:11, God said that His Word would accomplish His purpose, simply because it is *His* Word; there is nothing in the passage to indicate that a faulty faith will thwart His promises.

Although the creeds are a valuable resource, still there is no easy answer to the question of just who is the Bride, because it does not depend on whom we feel we should allow, but on whom *Jesus* allows and wants.

One Bride in All the Earth

> Next, I believe that there is one holy Christian Church on earth, i.e. the community or number or assembly of all Christians in all the world, the one bride of Christ, and his spiritual body of which he is the only head.
> Martin Luther[32]

> There is one Body and one Spirit, just as you were called to the one hope of your calling, one Lord, one faith, one Baptism, one God and Father of all, Who is over all and through all and in all.
> Ephesians 4:4-6

When denominations exclude each other from the celebration of Communion, yet both claim to be within the Bride of Christ, is this a heresy in deed? After all, there cannot be more than one Bride, one Body of Christ, unless St Paul is a liar. The past has been riddled with verbal, theological and even physical wars to expound "the correct" version of faith, yet Jesus accepted the disciples, even when they were appallingly in error in their understandings. How far can we go before what we say we profess ("one faith") becomes too much in conflict with what we then practice?

We Do Not Get to Choose

Both Luther and St Paul declare that Christians are one Body with only one Head, Jesus, and if all who are in Jesus are connected with Him as the Body of Christ, how can one say that he is "not in Communion," that is, not connected, with other Christians? – unless he insists that one, or the other, or both are not connected to Jesus, which according to the above may be a most difficult thing to prove. And if the "other" person meets the faith criteria recognized as defining what a Christian is, then there is no such thing as that Jesus is "not connected enough" with them.

If both are made one in Him [John 17:21-23], then it requires more than merely acknowledgement of some sort of commonality. Rather both would be compelled to seek how, as the Body of Christ, they must work together, each contributing their uniqueness, each seeking the other's giftedness to the goal of *upbuilding* the Body *in Love* [Ephesians 4:16] – and that does not mean just one's own part of the Body.

Who is Denied?

It is Jesus Who has washed His Bride with "water with the Word," that He might present her "to Himself in splendor …, that she might be holy and without blemish" [Ephesians 5:27]. With earnest desire, His delight, His joy is to feed His Bride at His Table. He is the One Who sets His Table; He is the One Who determines who qualifies as His Bride; He feeds even when we do not understand, grasp, or believe the way we ought to; He welcomes even those who would surprise *us*.

To deny the Table to someone whom *He* counts as His Bride *forbids Jesus from Communion, from feeding His Bride*! Should He wait apprehensively for us to decide who is fit for His Table? Should this not compel a bit of pause before we exclude someone? It would seem that the incident where the disciples prevented the little children from being touched by our Lord, "but when Jesus saw it, He was greatly displeased" [Mark 10:14] should apply here as well in regard to the 'little ones' of faith, no matter which denomination they are in.

He has washed and made spotlessly clean, to present His Bride to Himself in splendor – when is it dangerous to find fault and, in essence, tell the Lord that *His* work has not been not good enough?

> Who will lay an accusation against God's elect? It is God Who justifies; who is he who condemns? Christ Jesus is the One Who died – more – Who was raised up, ... Who also intercedes for us.   Romans 8:33-34

After describing the timeless, locationless and eternal quality of the oneness of the single Body of Christ in Communion, is it not a real problem to insist to the Bridegroom that part of His Bride shall not be welcome, and that His gift of Himself to them, even when defectively understood, must occur outside of what we will allow?

Stewards of the Mysteries of God

A Profound Responsibility

> So, therefore of us – let a man reckon us as servants of Christ and stewards of God's mysteries.   I Corinthians 4:1

> The Lord said, "Who then is the faithful and wise steward, whom the lord will set over his household, to distribute the food portions at the proper time?"   Luke 12:42

Jesus does entrust "the mysteries" of His gifts particularly to the Church's leadership as His stewards, who are charged "to distribute the food portions at the proper time." They are guardians of holy God-given treasures which are of life-and-death importance – this trust is an awesome privilege and responsibility. Many church bodies take this commission seriously, which they must.

A Serious Responsibility

The Dual Effect

> Forming light and creating darkness, making peace [*shalom*] and creating affliction – I am Jehovah, Who does all these things. Isaiah 45:7

> Because of Christ we are a sacrificially[33] pleasing odor to God in the ones being saved and in the ones perishing – to the one it is indeed the smell of death to death; to the other, the smell of life to life. ...
> II Corinthians 2:15-16

God's actions are two-edged: they bring salvation to those who yield to Him; they bring judgment to those who resist Him. Of the plagues that beset Egypt at the time of the Exodus, at the same time that they were wonderful affirmations of God's presence and salvation (to the Jews), they were also devastating judgments and calls to obedience (to the Egyptians). Had Pharaoh heeded the message of the plagues, who knows how that nation would have been blessed for generations to come. But Pharaoh's heart was hardened by God's activity [Exodus 4:21; 7:3] and therefore sounded the judgment knell for himself and his land.

His Word

> He who rejects Me and does not receive My words has one which judges him: the Word which I spoke – that will judge him on the last day. For I have not spoken from myself – the One Who sent Me, the Father Himself, commanded Me as to what I should say and what I should speak. And I know that His commandment is life eternal ....
> John 12:48-50

His Word – "He said so" – brings judgment or eternal life, depending on whether one rejects it or accepts it. Since *this* Word is what is connected to the Sacraments, along with the awesome message of salvation, these precious gifts are not to be treated flippantly, nor to be eroded in their significance. The Bride's task then is to instill a respect for and a consciousness of God's will, heart and command as found therein, and also to identify the grave and serious decision that faces the participant who rejects the Host.

A Limited Responsibility

"Doing God One Better"

In Genesis 3, the serpent strikes up a conversation with Eve, getting her to repeat God's command (an essential step to make sin *rebellion*). In verse 3, she adds to the command, "neither shall you touch it." God had not said that. But it is such a good and reasonable improvement on His command, that it "ought to be there"! Already the attitude that underlies sin is forming: I can "adjust" God's commands: after all, I have such worthwhile ideas, and when necessary, I can override God's will with something that is obviously more reasonable. Jesus struggles with the Jewish leaders concerning this:

> Woe also to you lawyers – because you yoke men with burdens hard to bear, but you yourselves do not touch the burdens with one of your fingers. Luke 11:46
>
> in vain they worship me, teaching as doctrine the laws of men.
> Matthew 15:9 (see Isaiah 29:13)

These passages hold both lesson and warning in regard to creating barriers and requirements that do not reflect the Bridegroom's earnest and desired gift to His Bride. Pharisees and lawyers in Jesus' day could point to history and to the desire to be holy for God in order to justify their additions, but

Jesus – the Bridegroom – is not impressed, not even by the nobleness of their intent.

The Master's Will

> Beyond that, it is necessary for stewards that each be found trustworthy.
> I Corinthians 4:2

John DeVries, founder of the World Home Bible League, once was climbing in the Canadian Rockies with his sons. When they reached a plateau, he had had enough. As he looked over the beautiful panorama before him, he began to laugh: "Lord, you made these mountains, the Andes, the Pyrenees, the Alps, mountains all over the world. I cannot even climb up one of them – and I am going to help YOU out?"

As with Baptism, our hands do the action in Communion, yet it is not our action – this sacrament is not something that belongs to us. Marking that distinction can be a struggle. A steward must only carry out the Master's will – he cannot assume authority beyond his charge; he cannot set standards that the Master has not set; he cannot define his responsibility in a way that expands outside his given assignment.

The Bridegroom's Feast

> I tell you, Something greater than the temple is here. Had you known what this means, "I desire mercy, and not sacrifice," you would not have condemned the guiltless. For Lord of the Sabbath is the Son of Man.
> Matthew 12:6-9

The Bridegroom is the "Lord of the Sabbath" – the Host of this Meal. It is centered on His Glory: His Goodness, His Covenant, His Grace, His

Mercy, His Justice [Exodus 33:19; 34:6-7]. It is He Who makes us "guiltless." The Bride is not the host but the steward of this Meal. So the Bride is to ensure that the Communion be treated with the respect and honor it deserves and that those whom Jesus counts as His Bride are freely welcomed, but to also warn of the ramifications to those who refuse the gift. How then should the Church fulfill this responsibility?

The Welcome Mat

> The Spirit and *the Bride* say, "Come!" ... Revelation 22:17

The Primary Action: To Invite

The primary action in this responsibility of *the Bride* is not to restrict but to invite. In fact, preaching the Word must be bound to the extraordinary offer of Grace and Love to be found in this Feast:

> For the preaching ought to be nothing but an explanation of the words of Christ when He instituted [Holy Communion] and said: "This is my body, this is my blood," etc. What is the whole gospel but an explanation of this testament? Christ has gathered up the whole gospel in a short summary with the words of this testament or sacrament. For the gospel is nothing but a proclamation of God's grace and of the forgiveness of all sins, granted us through the sufferings of Christ, as St. Paul proves in Romans 10, and as Christ says in Luke 24.
> Martin Luther[34]

Some Christian groups have as part of their service an "Altar Call" where one might receive prayer and blessing from the ministry in that congregation. But this is a far greater "Altar Call" when the Bridegroom Himself as Host beckons us to receive His very Self – to receive His everything. This is the summation of the Gospel with all that it contains, the natural conclusion to every message and every sermon.

Thirsty

We are familiar with the saying:

> You can lead a horse to water, but you cannot make him drink.

But then someone added the comment:

> however, you can feed him lots of salt!

> ... [O]ne should not bind any person with commandments or ordinances, or entice him toward the gospel with customs or with words; but one should preach freely and then let people come of their own accord and insist upon [Holy Communion].   Martin Luther[35]

What draws "Christians" to commune? It is not to be laws, customs or habit, but rather clear, consistent and constant preaching that creates a hunger and thirst for *Jesus* – and for what He offers.

> To this [Holy Communion] all those should come who hunger and thirst after this food, that is, all devout, believing Christians, contrite and fearful consciences who desire with all their hearts to become righteous and whole.   Martin Luther[36]

From the Highways and the By-Ways

But just how open should the Bride be with this invitation, "Come!"? Surely a random person should not be simply grabbed off the street and be brought to the Master's Table! Yet in the parable of the Wedding Feast in Matthew 22:1-14, the servants/messengers are told precisely to do that [vv 9-10 (emphasis mine)]:

"Go therefore into the crossroads of the highways, and as many as you find invite to the Marriage Feast." And having gone out into the highways, those servants gathered all which they found, *both evil and good*; so the wedding hall became full of guests.

Still it is also important that the guests do have the appropriate "dress":

> "Friend, how did you enter here without a wedding garment?"
> And he was speechless. v 12

The proper "dress"?

> For as many as were baptized into Christ, you have put on Christ
> Galatians 3:27
>
> But put on the Lord Jesus Christ... Romans 13:14

The proper dress is based simply upon Jesus – there is no other qualification. It is not the abundance of knowledge, the refined theology – those from the highways and by-ways likely have not gone through a thorough training session before being admitted to the Feast. They may be well-educated thinkers; some may be mentally challenged; some may simply be uneducated slaves, purposely kept ignorant – yet the desire is clearly

> I will greatly rejoice in Jehovah, my soul shall exult in my God; for *He* has clothed me with the garments of salvation, *He* has put on me the robe of righteousness, as a bridegroom wears a festive turban, and as a bride is adorned with her jewels. Isaiah 61:10

The Bride as a good steward, by her preaching and declaration of God's plan of salvation, provides a garment that is not a clothing of doctrine and information, but rather is the living Garment of the Lord of Life Himself, Who is the Bridegroom and the very Master of the Feast. Just as Jesus "cleansed her by the washing of water with the word" [Ephesians 5:26], so also Jehovah clothes us "with the garments of salvation ... the robe of righteousness."

Admission to the Feast is not based so much on *what* they know, but *Who* they know.

The Limited Unwelcome Mat

A Negative Side

Unfortunately there are times when this responsibility requires a negative action. When a person takes a path that will destroy himself, if not here then eternally, if Jesus cares, should not the Bride also care? There are times when the Bride must deny access to the table:

> *The only exception* is the person who desires no grace and absolution and has no intention to amend his life.
>
> Book of Concord[57] [emphasis mine]

In the late medieval-early renaissance world when the Book of Concord was written (1580), how thoroughly trained in doctrine were the believers who came to the Table? The discussion for "the only exception" revolves not around knowledge but in regard to refusing the Bridegroom and what He offers. What is difficult, though, is that we cannot look into a heart. Therefore the Bride must be very careful about responsibly handling this great power. It is not whether "they do not agree with us," or "we do not like them" or that "they are not one of us"; it is only about whether they *reject Jesus*, what He has done and is doing for them. Recognizing both Peter's (and Judas's?) presence at the Last Supper, we must allow for the struggling, fledgling faith as opposed to the one who simply discards the Bridegroom's Love.

The Toughest Responsibility

There are also times when Christians go into a tailspin in their morals:

> It is reported that there is actually immorality among you…. he who has done this deed should be removed from among you. Although absent in body, I am present in spirit, and as "present," I have already passed judgment on the man who has done this thing. In the Name of the Lord Jesus, when you are assembled, together with my spirit, with the power of our Lord Jesus, deliver such a one to Satan for the destruction of the flesh, that the spirit may be saved in the day of the Lord Jesus.
> I Corinthians 5:1, 3-5

When they embarrass and disgrace us (oh, uh, rather, *the Bridegroom* …), how easy it would be to reject them. But remember how the Bridegroom has taken each of *us* from the gutter and has washed *us* clean and makes *us* beautiful to Himself; what should our attitude be then toward a fellow sinner? Truly there is need for reprimands – not to reject, but to restore:

> Sufficient for such a one has been this punishment by the majority; so that now in contrast you should forgive and encourage him, lest such a one be overwhelmed by excessive grief. So I encourage you to confirm your Love toward him.   II Corinthians 2:6-8

> Brethren, if a man is overtaken in any trespass, you who are spiritual restore such a one in a spirit of gentleness, considering yourself lest you also be tempted. Bear one another's burdens, and so fulfill the law of Christ.   Galatians 6:1-2

The idea of the reprimand and the denial of a fellow Christian from the Table, is in regard to a blatant moral sin. When there is repentance, even when *our* sense of "justice" is not satisfied, there must be forgiveness – because the Bridegroom *already* has.

Denominational Friction

What about when denominations take a doctrinal or practical direction that is specifically against God's Word? The danger they fall into is equal to Israel and Judah during the time of the Kings: it is the attempt to worship somewhat at the feet of God, but also with a very decided lean toward other "gods." In today's world, often the challenge is whether to worship at the feet of social opinion as an authority equal to or even overriding God's Word. It is the danger of Eve's attitude that God's will can be "adjusted." With the Chosen People, such mixing of their worship earns them disciplinary captivity – which is not a pretty time.

How then should we react? The example of I Corinthians 5:1-6 is a necessary principle – there are times when one is forced to admit that some do walk a path that rejects God's will, and as responsible stewards we must draw attention to the fact that *a spiritual separation from Jesus* has occurred.

The Terrible Dilemma

It is a terrible dilemma when a church body says that it ascribes to the faith as described in the creeds yet disobeys the Lordship of the Bridegroom. What then are we to do?

The Bride must guard herself from the temptation to pray as the Pharisee did, "God, I thank You that I am not like …" [Luke 18:11]. Instead, her heart must always seek to reflect the heart of the Bridegroom. We may reject what some may be *doing*, but we cannot reject the people. They may be Peters and even Judases, but what would – did – does – Jesus do?

Luther had said, as quoted before, in extending what happens in infant Baptism: *"Nor should I doubt that even a godless adult could be changed, in any of the sacraments, if the same church prayed for and presented him."* We are confronted with the question whether this Means of Grace really does have power to create faith, or whether it lies in the realm of the merely symbolic – is Jesus really present, and does He accomplish His will?

At the same time, there is the reality that sin's rebellion simply hardens when it meets God's action (as Pharaoh's heart had in Exodus 7:13; 8:15). Our decision cannot, however, be based on whether they merely disagree with us. The determination must be based on whether they are intentionally rejecting the Lordship of the Host of the Table, meanwhile as we retain the humility of knowing that we are not perfect followers of the Bridegroom ourselves.

This situation demands that we end up at the feet of Jesus, seeking His wisdom and understanding, recognizing that His Word has authority, calling on the Holy Spirit to be at the center of this situation. How comforting it is to know that as we pray from the depths of our hearts according to His will, it will indeed echo the intensity of the intercession from the depths of our Lord's Spirit [Romans 8:26-27] and His heart [Romans 8:34].

The Final Responsibility

However, aside from those special cases, for most people the ultimate responsibility lies not with the observer/steward, but within each recipient:

Therefore, let this irrefutable truth stand fast: Where there is a divine promise, there every one must stand on his own feet; his own personal faith is demanded, he will give an account for himself and bear his own load [Gal 6:5]; as it is said in the last chapter of Mark [16:16]: "he who believes and is baptized will be saved; but he who does not believe will be condemned." Martin Luther[38]

There is push and pull to communing: the push comes from the realization of one's weakness and the sins that bother the conscience; but the pull is the presence of our Beloved Bridegroom, His invitation, and what of Himself He so graciously, eagerly gives. The precious table of Holy Communion is continually laid out in worship and Word, so that all may be drawn to it, desire it, and discover the joy of the Bridegroom as He feeds His Beloved Bride. The ultimate decision lies between the potential communicant's heart and his Lord. When he is drawn and comes looking for this inexpressible gift of Jesus, then as good stewards we must "distribute the food portions at the proper time," because of such is the utter delight of the Lord of the Feast.

9. The Reluctant Bride

The Loving Meal

The Bridegroom sits next to His Beloved. She is the total focus of His attention as He feeds her. Although He has had no illusions, she now has become exactly what He saw she would be. And His Love is unbounded.

She on the other hand is so centered on Him. Amazement is mixed with Love, joy is mixed with humility. Her whole field of vision is now focused on her Beloved Bridegroom. She knows what she had once been, without Him, and she knows what she now is because of Him. Formerly she literally was nothing, but now it is "all Him."

No Longer the Exuberance of Love

Someone Moved

Back when the front seat of a car was still a bench seat, a wife mentioned to her husband, who was driving, that when they first went together, they used to snuggle together as they traveled. Now they sit at both ends of the seat. The husband replied, "Well, *I* have not moved!"

The Bride Moves Away

What's this?? What's happened?? The Bride has drawn away! No longer does she immerse herself in her Beloved's abundant Love. No longer does she rejoice in His closeness. No longer is His opinion her single most important focus. No longer is the Bride centered on the Bridegroom.

She has become self-conscious, preoccupied with herself. Perhaps she should not be so eager – as a sinner, modesty might dictate she should not be so bold. Perhaps the Beloved should work a little harder for her attention. Perhaps she should come to the Bridegroom's Table only when she feels appropriately ready.

Echoes of Adam and Eve

This is a characteristic of sin! In the beginning, Adam and Eve gave no thought about themselves. Their total focus and total enjoyment were upon God and they only saw themselves reflected in His eyes. But sin made them preoccupied with themselves. They were looking for what benefits were in it for themselves. God was Someone to hide from, One Who justifiably could condemn them. They saw themselves naked – having nothing with which to cover their inadequacies. Similarly the Bride's eyes are no longer on the Bridegroom Who Loves her so dearly.

Reduced Intimacy

Fear Rules

Wretched

> I do not understand what I end up doing: what I want is not what I do; but what I hate, this I do ... I know that nothing good dwells within me (this is in my flesh). The will is in me, but I cannot *do* what is right. For the good I wish to do, I do not practice; however the evil I do not want, *this* is what I do ... Wretched man that I am! Who will deliver me from this body of death? Romans 7:15, 18-19, 24

The Bride finds herself struggling against sin – and losing. She hesitates – how could the Bridegroom ever accept her? He is One Who justifiably could condemn her.

> There is no fear in the Love [*agape*]; but perfect Love casts out the fear, *because the fear has torment, and he who fears has not been made perfect in the Love.*
> I John 4:18 (Emphasis mine)

Because the Bridegroom does not fill her vision, because she is absorbed with herself, anxiety, fear, and torment stand in the way of a once-loving relationship.

Worthy

The Worthy "Unworthy"?

She is worried. How could one as sinful as she ever be worthy of the attentions of the holy Great God of the universe, the Bridegroom Himself? What St Paul says about unworthiness fills her with apprehension:

> So then, whoever eats the Bread or drinks the Cup of the Lord unworthily will be guilty of the Body and Blood of the Lord.
> I Corinthians 11:27

But then Luther insists that only the *unworthy* are worthy:

> [T]he highest wisdom is to realize that this sacrament does not depend upon our worthiness. We are not baptized because we are worthy and holy, nor do we come to confession pure and without sin; on the contrary we come as poor, miserable men, precisely because we are unworthy. The only exception is the person who desires no grace and absolution and has no intention to amend his life.   *Book of Concord*[39]

Those who are worthy are the ones who are unworthy ... only the unworthy are worthy ... this can sure be confusing! If we are to partake in a worthy manner (so said Paul), how do we do this?

The Unworthy "Worthy"?

> Without this faith, whatever else is brought to it by way of prayers, preparations, works, signs, or gestures are incitements to impiety rather than exercises of piety. It usually happens that those who thus prepared imagine themselves legitimately entitled to approach the altar, when in reality they are less prepared than at any other time or by any other work, because of the unbelief they bring with them.   Martin Luther[40]

To try to make oneself worthy can actually end up in the opposite direction?? Yes. When the Bride looks into herself as if the Sacrament's power somehow comes through her fitness, her activity, her ritual, her methodology, her "worthiness," she trusts in the wrong thing ("because of their unbelief"): she trusts in herself.

The Real "Worthy"

It is the Bridegroom alone Who has chosen His Bride, Who has washed her, Who has made her (spiritually) beautiful; *He alone establishes her worthiness*. To eat and drink in a worthy manner means that only one item is brought to the Table:

> So if you would receive this sacrament and testament worthily, see to it that you give emphasis to these living words of Christ, rely on them with a strong faith, and desire what Christ has promised you in them: then it will be yours, then you will be worthy and well prepared.
>   Martin Luther[41]

Simply put, the Bride comes because God has invited her, because she *believes* His invitation.

> Since, then, [Holy Communion] is nothing else than a testament, the first and by far the best preparation for it is truly a hungry soul and a firm and joyful faith of the heart which accepts such a testament. ... But if you have letter and seal [His promise and testament], and believe, desire, and seek it, it must be given to you, even though you were scaly, scabby, stinking and most filthy. Martin Luther[42]

She comes because she knows that He has washed her and has given to her His own righteousness. She needs Him, she wants Him, and here He is. She has "in hand" His promises, His Word – His invitation – and her faith. She cannot be denied.

Gratitude

> If to him it was not an unworthy thing to bequeath so great a sum to an unworthy person, why should I refuse to accept it because of my unworthiness? Indeed, it is for this very reason that I cherish all the more his unmerited gift – because I am unworthy! With that same thought every man ought to fortify his conscience against all qualms and scruples, so that he may lay hold on the promise of Christ with unwavering faith, and take the greatest care to approach the sacrament not trusting in confession, prayer, and preparation, but rather, despairing of all these, with firm confidence in Christ who gives the promise. For, as we have said often enough, the word of promise must reign alone here in pure faith; such faith is the one and only sufficient preparation.
> Martin Luther[43]

The Bridegroom, His Word and His gifts, are the center of focus, not the Bride's worthiness or unworthiness. The Bridegroom's Table is a gift precisely for *sinners* such as you and I. What then of preparations and the rest? Properly used, they can enhance the appreciation of the Sacrament.

But they also may divert our faith toward our own efforts, and therefore must be regarded as having great risk when used.

Renewal

Confession

Luther said in the above quote:

> ... not trusting in confession, prayer, and preparation, but rather, despairing of all these, with firm confidence in Christ who gives the promise. ...

But is not confession of sins supposed to be essential? Yes, it is necessary to remove the clutter of sin clouding the face of the Beloved. It is necessary to be turned back around in our attitudes and thinking. It is necessary to not hold on to what God will destroy forever, that is, our sin.

However, humans can seem to change almost anything into a work-righteousness, where we "earn the right" – or attempt to compel God to bless us – based upon our earnestness or preciseness or comprehensiveness or whatever may be the thing that we personally happen to excel in. As with preparations, even confession can be an "incitement to unbelief," where one's trust is more in his endeavor to influence God to forgive, than in the Bridegroom's earnest desire and action by which He is already offering forgiveness. As mentioned before, it is in that offer of forgiveness that we find the freedom and confident hope which allows us to confess even those things of which we are most ashamed.

Restoration

So is it wrong to face the sin in our lives and confess it? By no means! However, we can become preoccupied with it. It can dominate our relationship to the Beloved, it can make us focus on ourselves – how bad we are, or how good we are, or how impressively we deal with our sin, or even how we may re-enjoy by recounting our sin – but the Bridegroom's desire is that we simply just be *rid* of the sin.

This is what Luther meant when He spoke of "daily renewing our Baptism," that is, to experience daily that re-creation by Jesus Who washes us yet again, in His pure joy of seeing His Bride emerge once more in all the glory and beauty He has given her. Of such is His forgiveness that since *He* remembers the sins no more [Jeremiah 31:34; Hebrews 8:12; 10:17], then with St Paul we also can be "forgetting what lies behind and straining forward to what lies ahead" [Philippians 3:13].

Although we must mean it when we hand over our sin in confession, this washing comes not because of measuring up to some earnestness level. What compels God to have had our forgiveness already prepared for the last two thousand years is *His heart*. The Bride does not have to persuade her Beloved to forgive her!!

St Paul's Abused Warning

Shouldn't We Fear This Feast?

> "… as often as you drink it, do this into remembrance of Me." For as often as you eat this Bread and drink the Cup, you proclaim the Lord's death until He comes. Therefore, whoever eats the Bread or drinks the Cup of the Lord unworthily will be guilty of the Body and Blood of the

Lord. Let a man examine himself, and so eat of the Bread and drink of the Cup.

For he who eats and drinks judgment ("damnation" KJV) upon himself eats and drinks without discerning the Body. Because of this, many among you are weak and ill, and many have died. But if we discerned ourselves, we should not be judged. And when being judged by the Lord, we are disciplined so that we should not be condemned with the world.

So then, my brothers, when you come together to eat, wait for one another ...   I Corinthians 11:25-31

Especially when the King James Version upped the ante by using the word "damnation" (which really is not appropriate in this passage), St Paul's words at times have been used to terrify the Bride, making her afraid whether she is participating worthily. In one fell swoop, the joy and delight of two who are deeply in Love which marks this Feast suddenly evaporates. Fear now rules. But is this really what the Apostle intended?

Contexts, Contexts

As always, any passage in the Bible cannot be torn from its context. Just prior to this, Paul denounces something that the Corinthians are doing:

> As well, in this responsibility I do not applaud you, because when you come together it is not for the better but for the worse. In the first place, when you come together in Church, I hear that there are divisions among you ... When you come together, it is not to eat the Lord's Supper among yourselves. For each first eats his own meal, so one is left hungry and another is drunk.   I,11:17-18,20-21

Cliques, divisions and factions are rife within the community, particularly when they gather together "as the Church." A prime example of the selfishness that reigns among them is the Agape (God's Love) Meal which they practice before the Communion. The result is that some are overfed while others go hungry, because it is no "potluck" (a sharing of what one has with everybody), but rather a "brown-bagged" meal (each is concerned only with himself and his own circle of people).

What an absolute perversion of the concept of Agape (God's special Love) and of what the Bride is all about! It is utterly disgraceful ("profaning"[44]) to the Lord Jesus' death (v 26) and to His presence. In contrast, in verses 23-25, St Paul sets before them Jesus' giving of Himself totally and without reservation, without pride or arrogance – the Bridegroom giving Himself – His total Self – to His Bride in the Communion.

Discerning the Body

It is interesting to note:

eat this Bread and drink the Cup	v 26
eats the Bread or drinks the Cup… the Body and Blood of the Lord	v 27
eat of the Bread and drink of the Cup	v 28

Why then is "the Blood" omitted in the following verse?

eats and drinks without discerning the Body	v 29

As has been mentioned before, and especially in I Corinthians, for Paul the term "the Body," when used by itself, is simply the Church, the "one Body" into which we have been Baptized [12:13]. Here in verse 29, the word for "discerning" ("*discerning* the Body") is also used in v 31 ("But if we *discerned* ourselves"), where the word "ourselves" is not "*for* ourselves" (the dative case), but rather it is the direct object (the accusative case) of "discerned" (in parallel to "the Body" in v 29). In other words, in "discerning the Body," we are recognizing *ourselves*: who we are and what we are to be about as Christ's Body – that is, that the presence of Jesus is in us in this place.

Therefore Paul's emphasis is not so much in regard to the Bread or the Body on the Altar, but rather that they are not discerning the Body that surrounds them and of which they are a part.

Paul deals with another, similar point of division in chapter 12: everybody has different gifts through the Holy Spirit, yet these gifts are thought of in regard to pride, and then are used to put others – or oneself – down, thereby crippling the Church. This focusing upon one's self fails to realize how each is only part of the greater whole, and that when each is contributing his gifts then the Body functions as it should. As the culmination of his argument, he continues into his "Love chapter" as "the more excellent way" for the Body to work smoothly together.

Results

> For as often as you eat this Bread and drink the Cup, you proclaim the Lord's death until He comes. [11:26]

Paul identifies that participation in Communion proclaims the salvation event – Jesus' death! But their practice destroys this proclamation – *they are not being the Bride*, instead they are being little worlds unto themselves. This is a manner most unworthy of the Bride of Christ, most unworthy of the Sacrament, and especially most unworthy of the Bridegroom Who has invested Himself so totally in others, in which this Communion-Connectedness is the result.

In being *dis*connected from the Source of Love [Chapter 13], no wonder they are experiencing weakness, sickness, and even death – because they are not caring for each other! The condemnation they experience is a self-condemnation; but in God's hands it is a disciplinary condemnation. They are not being packed off to hell, they are just being turned around.

Therefore "if we discerned ourselves" – who we really are, or rather who the Bridegroom has made us – then "we would not be judged" – we would not receive the discipline [11:32] of the Lord. This is *discipline*, not *damnation* – the King James translators missed the point.

The Unworthy Manner

> God bless me and my wife,
> Son John and his wife,
> Us four, no more.

The Corinthians have acted as though Holy Communion is merely for each's own benefit, that is, "my faith is just between me and God and nobody else"; they have not been ashamed of the politics and power plays that strip the Church of the potency to be found in this Sacrament. But most of all, the Bridegroom has been treated as incidental, merely a rubber stamp for their notions, conclusions, and desires.

Therefore comes St Paul's final comment, "*So then*, when you come together to eat, wait for one another …" [v 33] – that is, it is time now to BE the Bride of Christ that you are: demonstrate His Love, pay attention to each other, care about each other, be the unified, strong, blessed – and powerful – Bride He has made you.

On the other hand, "Let God be true though every man be false" [Romans 3:4] – despite human shenanigans, the Bridegroom has never been other than true to HIS nature: still He comes, still He gives Himself totally, still He forgives, still He enters, still He touches His Bride's life, still He works within and through each person.

Pride Blocks

Let's Have Lunch

A slot of time in the husband's day has become available. He calls his wife and says, "Let's have lunch together at the restaurant's buffet." Her reaction is: (Pick one)

>a. "I would love to! I shall leave right now and meet you there."

>b. "You should have told me this last night! I have not fully, emotionally prepared myself to meet you right now!"

>c. "I cannot! I would have to figure out what to wear and put on my make-up; I do not have enough time to get ready! I just cannot meet you the way I am at the drop of a hat!"

The Bridegroom speaks to His Bride,

>With fervent desire I have desired to eat this [Meal] with you …
>
>Luke 22:15

He looks forward to having some special time together. *Her* reaction is …

I'm Not Ready Yet

Is it not stylish for the Bride to keep her Suitor waiting? She has not "properly" prepared herself – she has not primped and preened enough! After all, she requires time "to make herself beautiful!" – yet it is the Bridegroom that has made her beautiful – even so, she is telling the God of

109

the Universe (Who is already here, eagerly awaiting her), "Sorry, You have to wait until I'm 'good' and 'ready'!"

There is no joyful running to the arms of the Beloved, Who has come just for her. Although the Bridegroom has no hesitation and no reservation to be here in this dinner just for her, she does not simply delay, she may even refuse to join Him if she feels she is not "properly ready" for Him.

The Scarlet O'Hara Syndrome

Scarlet O'Hara in the movie version of Gone with the Wind was so self-absorbed that she could not recognize true love until it was too late. Rather than the delight of the shared love in front of her, she chased after an unrealistic goal, preening and primping for an imagined ideal.

She looked past the one who deeply loved her for exactly who she was. When she finally did truly turn to him, he who had loved her was so disillusioned that he had given up. Our Bridegroom never gives up on the relationship, but how much does His Bride tax His patience, turning away from His deep Love which He wants to share right now in such a very real and personal way?

Too Often

"Familiarity breeds contempt"

This saying is ridiculous in the eyes of deep and abiding Love. If that were so, then people should never get married, despite how God uses marriage to describe His relationship to us! The intent of newlyweds is to spend even more time with each other, to start the morning in the Beloved's presence, to close the day in the Beloved's presence, to literally be part of the Beloved's each day – to look up from the Supper Table and see the Beloved's face.

How Often?

> Likewise He also took the cup after supper, saying, "This cup is the new Covenant in My Blood; as often as you drink it, do this into remembrance of Me." For as often as you eat this Bread and drink the Cup, you proclaim the Lord's death until He comes.
> I Corinthians 11:25-26

How often is enough? The answer is determined by Love:

> If we see someone once a year and that is too often, that says something about our love for him.

> If we see someone once a month and it is just often enough, that says something about our love for him.

> If we see someone every day and it is not often enough, that says something about our love for him.

First and foremost, the frequency of coming to the Table with the Beloved should be founded upon Love, especially the extraordinary Love and joy of the *Bridegroom* for His Beloved.

> He has brought me to the banquet hall, and his banner over me is Love.
> Song of Solomon 2:4

If we were to have the Sacrament every day, He would still prepare His Table wholeheartedly, enthusiastically for His Beloved – the Beloved for whom He broke through every obstacle. Never has He ever even hinted at reluctance, no matter how often we may seek this fellowship. What is His heart-felt desire in regard to this meal with His Bride? – again, "with fervent desire I have desired to eat … with you" [Luke 22:15].

"Leprosy"

Insensitivity

Often leprosy is thought of as something that causes the fingers and other parts of the body to fall off. But that is only an indirect result from this disease. Actually what leprosy does is that it kills the nerves: it silences the system that warns the body of danger, injury and infection. A person can have an open wound, and he does not know it. It can become infected, and he does not know it. It can become gangrenous and literally rot off – and he does not know it.

It is a living death. In the Old Testament, leprosy is one of the few diseases specifically mentioned, because spiritually, sin is like leprosy, making us insensitive or desensitized. No longer are we aware of the open wound of our sin nor do we see the destruction it creates nor the death it brings.

Spiritually Insensitive

An individual grows cold and callous toward the Bridegroom of his soul and toward the rest of the Bride. No longer does he recognize the death that attacks the extremities of his life. He feels no need or usefulness to join the Bridegroom at His Table.

> If therefore, you are heavy-laden and feel your weakness, then go joyfully to this Sacrament and obtain refreshment, consolation, and strength…

But if you say: What, then, shall I do if I cannot feel such distress or experience hunger and thirst for the Sacrament? Answer: For those who are so minded that they do not realize their condition, I know no better counsel than that they put their hand into their bosom to ascertain whether they also have flesh and blood. And if you find that to be the case, then go, for your good, to St. Paul's Epistle to the Galatians, and hear what sort of a fruit your flesh is: [chap. 5, 19ff.] …

Therefore, if you cannot feel it, at least believe the Scriptures, they will not lie to you and they know your flesh better than you yourself… But that we do not feel it is so much the worse; for it is a sign that this is a leprous flesh which feels nothing, and yet [the leprosy] rages and keeps spreading. Yet as we have said, if you are quite dead to all sensibility, still believe the Scriptures, which pronounce sentence upon you. And, in short, the less you feel your sins and infirmities, the more reason have you to go to the Sacrament to seek help and a remedy.   Martin Luther[45]

No Good Reason

According to Luther: there is no good reason to stay away when the Bridegroom offers His total Self. If you feel your sin, then come! If you do not feel your sin, then the situation is desperate – all the more reason to come! If you feel bogged down and overwhelmed in life, then come! If you eagerly enjoy the Lord, then come! – simply COME!

> The Spirit and *the Bride* say, *"Come!"* He who hears, let him say, *"Come!"* And he who thirsts, let him *come.* He who chooses, let him take the water of life freely.   Revelation 22:17
>
> All whom the Father gives Me will come to Me, and the one who comes to Me I will *never* cast out.   John 6:37

As Ambrose of Milan said of the Eucharist, "Because I always sin, I always need to take the medicine."

Enjoyment

Besides, apparently Jesus just likes to be with us. There is nothing that He feels He would rather be doing, other than spending His time with His Bride. His Supper is by His earnest desire and by His invitation. All this simply, merely because, in His great Love for His Bride, He wants to share Himself especially in this way.

> No matter how, or where, or under what circumstances;
> no matter how "so frequent," or "not well attended";
> no matter how sudden, or how "unprepared" we are;
> He will be here *every single time* whenever the Feast is prepared.

There is nowhere any lack of enthusiasm, any shadow of inconvenience, any hint of annoyance from Jesus' direction. If there is any reluctance at having Communion, it certainly is not on His part – *He* has not moved to other end of the seat.

When He "prepares His Table before me" [Psalm 23:5], how should the Bride react?

10. Tangible Love

The Key Nature of Love

Love *Must* Give Itself

> What does Love always desire? Love does not ask for gifts. Love asks for Love. "I don't want your gifts" says the maid to the lover, "I want you." Why this? Because Love must always give itself to and for the Beloved. If Love were to give anything else but Love, it would not be real Love. Now this little baby in Bethlehem is God. It is Love, it is God giving Himself.
> ... When we realize that God is Love, Bethlehem must follow. ... Because God is Love, Love had to give itself. It did give itself. The Child in Bethlehem was born because God loved the world.
> Berthold von Schenk[46]

The precious Birth in Bethlehem is the reality – the inevitable conclusion – of Love giving Itself. This is no less the framework within which Holy Communion occurs. The concreteness of Bethlehem and the concreteness of Holy Communion *must* occur: God *must* give Himself.

Tangible Presence

Some argue that the spiritual should be solely adequate for us – why do we need the physical elements? Is not dependence on a physical token actually a sign of the lack of faith? But God created mankind as physical creatures as well! Bethlehem reveals that words are not enough *for the Bridegroom* – all the words of the prophets, all the messages from God Himself, could not replace the Baby in the manger. The Bridegroom is not ashamed to deal with us on a physical level – He is unafraid that His Bride should actually touch and be touched by her Beloved.

Look at My hands and My feet. It is I Myself! Touch Me and see...
Luke 24:39

But what about after His Ascension? How could He maintain such closeness?

> ... I sought him whom my soul loves; I sought him, but I did not find him [I called him, but he gave no answer]* I will rise now and go about the city, in the streets and in the plazas; I will seek him whom my soul loves. I sought him, but found him not.
> Song of Solomon 3:1-2 [*RSV includes]

How can that reality of His Self-giving that caused Bethlehem, be continued to every generation following?

Love Giving Itself Continuously

"This is My Body... This is My Blood ..." These statements are entirely consistent with Bethlehem. These statements are entirely consistent with the giving of Love. Again, *to the Bridegroom*, words are not enough.

He is the One Who desires this physical reality in giving of Himself. He has given His Bride something tangible because it is His joy to do so. Certainly Holy Communion requires no more impossible and extraordinary work of God than when God the Son "emptied" Himself to be found in human form [Philippians 2:5].

The same power that caused the Bridegroom to be found in physical form has made Him be attached to physical form once again. That power is His Love for His Bride, so that He might give Himself to His Beloved.

Touchable, Substantial Love

Why Physical?

Why does the Bridegroom have to go to all this trouble? After all, how important are the physical elements anyway, since the essential keystone for receiving Holy Communion is faith?

> I can enjoy the sacrament in [Holy Communion] every day if I only keep before my eyes the testament, that is, the words and promise of Christ, and feed and strengthen my faith on them.   Martin Luther[47]

> For he who desires it and believes, receives it spiritually, as St. Augustine teaches.   Martin Luther[48]

Is it not merely to reassure those of weak faith, that therefore the physical elements are required?

"With fervent desire I have desired to eat ... with you"
[Luke 22:15]

> A faithful, God-fearing heart does this: it asks first whether it is God's Word. When it hears that it is, it smothers with hands and feet the question why it is useful or necessary. For it says with fear and humility, "My dear God, I am blind; truly I know not what is useful or necessary for me, nor do I wish to know, but I believe and trust that thou dost know best and dost intend the best in thy divine goodness and wisdom. I am satisfied and happy to hear thy simple Word and perceive thy will."
>   Martin Luther[49]

Moreover since God has instituted this sacrament, we must not despise it, but receive it with great reverence, praise and gratitude. For if there were no other reason why we should observe [Holy Communion] outwardly and not be satisfied with inward faith alone, then this is reason enough, that God so instituted and wills it. And His will ought to please us above all things and should be sufficient reason to do or to omit anything. Martin Luther[50]

This meal is what the Bridegroom chooses to give us. It is His earnest eagerness, His joy, His self-giving – it is something He really wants to do. If He thinks we need it, then we need it more than we can ever realize. How then should His Beloved respond but to joyfully come – because this is the Bridegroom's delight!

Powerful Imagery!

Empowering Imagery

The Bread and Wine enter our bodies as natural food. The unchangeably-holy Creator enters a sinful human creature, yet His holiness is not violated, nor does it by rights destroy us! The physical food enters the bloodstream and then into the cells of the body – becoming part of the cells and empowering them for living. The Bridegroom enters, becoming one with His Bride [John 6:56; 14:6], empowering her for Life [John 10:10].

He withholds nothing, not His Body nor His Blood – He gives Himself "body and soul" to His Beloved. On the Cross He gave Himself *for* His Bride, but in Holy Communion, He gives Himself *to* His Bride. This is Grace, Forgiveness and Love all wrapped up into a single significant act. What greater proof of Forgiveness – and His Love – could God give, but that He would fearlessly join Himself to sinners such as we!

Telltale Imagery

Here is the amazement of Bethlehem: the Bridegroom has come to woo His Bride, as the Eternal God Himself joins to Humanity, unmistakably, physically, forever.

Here is the impact of Good Friday: this is the Body broken, the Blood spilled, because the Bridegroom would not settle for being parted from His Bride forever.

Here is the victory of Easter: Sunday worship is the weekly celebration of Him Who is the Resurrection [John 11:25], where the Bridegroom has destroyed the barriers that have kept His Bride from Him and reaffirms the tangibility of His Love ("handle Me and see" that I am alive [Luke 24:39]).

Here is the proclamation of the Ascension: when Jesus did not go to retire but to empower, putting into reality His plan where He would always be with His Bride "until the end of the age."

Here is the anticipation of the Grand Feast in Heaven: when the Bridegroom calls for His Beloved to now join Him in the home He has prepared, where the waiting and yearning will all be past.

Effectively, powerfully, wonderfully God drives home the essential points of His Gospel – here is Grace, Mercy, Forgiveness, Life, Hope – put into an unmistakable presentation of His Love.

Concrete Imagery

Why would the Bridegroom so arrange it this way? Because this physical evidence of Communion is powerful: the Bride can time and again come to an event in history, an actual time and place in which the

Bridegroom physically confirms His promises, His intentions, His involvement. It is His demonstration of:

You have cast behind Your back all my sins	Isaiah 38:17
See, I am with you all the days to the end of the age	Matthew 28:20
He makes all things work together for good	Romans 8:28
where I am, you also will be	John 14:3
no created thing can separate us from the Love of God	Romans 8:39

She can be absolutely confident because the Bridegroom has fed her with His very Self, so that there is no mistaking, no misgiving, no questioning, no wondering. Constant sharing of Himself is simply His utter delight and joy – after all, He deeply Loves His Bride and wants to be with her. And His Bride deeply loves Him and wants to be with Him.

The Key Nature of the Words

Imagery or Reality?

> If anyone Loves Me, he will keep My Word, and My Father will Love him; We will come to him and will make Our dwelling with him.
> John 14:23

> the Spirit of the Truth… you know Him, because He dwells with you, and will be in you.
> John 14:17

"We will make Our dwelling with him" – we do not physically see it; most often we do not feel it; we do not understand how this can be. How then can it be true? Yet Jesus says this is what God does. Not figuratively – but really. Faith simply takes the Lord at His Word.

Simple Words

Suppose Jesus really does want to give us His very Own Body and Blood. What words should He use – other than the simple, clean, matter-of-fact: "This is My Body...This is My Blood"? These simple words "This is..." attaches concreteness to imagery, the spiritual to some thing – the Bread and the Wine – which employs the physical senses: hearing, sight, smell, touch, taste – all which God Himself has created in us.

Certainly a Love that could combine human and divine in Bethlehem would have no problem making these words just as real as "Lo, I am with you always." If this is what He wants to do for His Bride, how else could He say it?

Symbolic Words

The trap of dealing with the spiritual world at the same time as the physical is that we often think of the physical as merely a symbolic aid. Since the Bread and the Wine do not visibly change into flesh and blood, therefore, it would seem, these physical objects are merely symbolic.

In a sense that is undeniable. But is that enough, in a religion in which spiritual reality overlays and combines with the physical – again culminating especially in that birth in Bethlehem? The physical Jesus is in a sense symbolic of "the dwelling of God is with men" (Revelation 21:3) – "Immanuel ('God is with us')" [Matthew 1:23]. In fact, that is the way that many people do think of Him, that He only represents/symbolizes a god-likeness in this world.

Yes, that is true, but He also is far, far more than that: He *is* God, not just merely a symbol of Him.

"Is"

The Significant Word

The apple "is" red. The apple symbolizes red? It can do that, however an apple can also be many other colors, but this apple actually is red. Let us say it a different way: The color of the apple is…. The apple is colored…. There just is no replacement for the plain word "is" in a description.

To define "is" as merely to "symbolize" of "signify" would rob ourselves of the ability to simply describe – and to describe simply. "This is My Body … This is My Blood" – must He really need to say it any differently? And if He does, would we even then be satisfied?

The Significance of "Is" With Jesus

"I Am"

"Is" has importance not only with the "This is …" statements, it has significance with Jesus' "I Am" statements as well. "Am" is just a different form of "is" – only the person as subject is different ("I" as opposed to "he," "she," or "it").

Jesus said, "I am the Resurrection" [John 11:25] – often people mentally change His meaning to: "I have the power of the Resurrection" or "I give the Resurrection" or even "I demonstrate the Resurrection" – in some way He merely *symbolizes* the Resurrection.

But the power of Jesus' statement is that the Resurrection is identical / synonymous to Himself. Put "Resurrection" wherever Jesus' Name is found, and vice versa because they are the same thing! When Jesus is "in our midst" [Matthew 18:20] – the Resurrection is in our midst! (a wonderful concept for funerals). *That is the significance of the word "is"!*

More *"I Am"'s*

I am the Life	NOT I only symbolize/show life
I am the Way.	NOT I only symbolize/show a way
I am the Truth	NOT I only symbolize/show a truth
I am the Bread of Life ..	NOT I only symbolize/show life-sustaining food

... and so on

Robbing "is" of its power destroys the potency of these statements. If Jesus only symbolizes Life, then He merely represents a vague hope for "life." He could not be "the Way," He merely demonstrates perhaps one of the ways to God. He only symbolizes truth since other religions have "truth" in them. What is disturbing is that this is exactly where some theologies do end up: Jesus is only a symbol, rather than in His Person is concrete reality.

Such theologies are awash with emptiness. Jesus' words and saving work have no force, no substance to them. There is no meat and bone to give shape to the ethereal words.

This is why the word "is" has such consequence!

Uncomplicated Truth

Spiritual Mystery

To conform spiritual mysteries into what humans can comprehend robs Jesus of His uncomplicated truth – uncomplicated to Him, though bewildering to us. Bethlehem reminds us that "with God every Word will not be impossible" [Luke 1:37].

His simple words tell us that Holy Communion – very obviously Bread and Wine – now has something extraordinary directly attached to these elements: the Bridegroom Himself is now present in a very special way, purely for the sake of His Bride. The Feast is Himself. It is a physical gift given because Jesus chooses to do it this way, and therefore we need it as He gives it. This is Love giving Himself yet again in a concrete reality – and Love receiving such a gift.

In, With, and Under

The Church has struggled with defining how Jesus is connected to the Bread and the Wine. Some speak of the physical elements as completely changed into His Body and Blood despite appearances. Some think the elements only symbolize and represent Jesus.

The third concept is that the physical elements remain what they are, however Jesus connects Himself "in, with, and under ("undergirds"? "lies under the surface appearance"?)" the Bread and the Wine. "In, with, and under" not only describes Jesus' presence with the Bread and Wine, it also describes *us* as we go forth with Jesus "in, with, and under" us. We are not changed into Jesus, nor are we just symbols of Him. He truly is in us, He has become one with us and we with Him, He "undergirds," is "just under the surface" of all we are now to do, say, think, etc.

> For My Flesh truly is food, and My Blood truly is drink. He who eats My Flesh and drinks My Blood abides in Me, and I in him.
> John 6:55-56

Intimacy

A Loaf of Bread, a Bottle of Wine, and Thou

"A loaf of bread, a bottle of wine, and thou" has long suggested intimacy. Here is the candlelit supper (remember, candles on the altar?), and over a simple meal, is the message "you are enough, all I would ever want or need." The two deeply in Love gaze at each other. This is no one night stand (although an eternal-day stand).

Sigh... Well, so much for the romantic mood...

But the picture, again and again, is that the central pivot of Communion is Love, a deep Love, an abiding Love, a self-giving Love, a mutual Love, and the delight each has in the other.

The One Loaf

An ancient Communion prayer sets the significance of the Bread this way:

> And praying that as this bread was once scattered upon the mountains, and is here gathered into one, so also gather Thy whole Church out of every nation, and every city and village and home and make one holy, living Church ...

Imagine the poor wheat, torn from the stalk, pounded in the threshing, ground in the mill, squeezed in the kneading, and *then* they turn up the heat. But oh, the aroma! When the loaf comes out of the oven, all these little individual grains of wheat now have been joined with each other into something most delightful. It is not the individual grain of wheat that makes the Bread so enjoyable; it is how each has joined each other to make a greater whole.

In the Bride, the individuals are to be so connected with each other so as to indeed be "one Loaf," which Bridegroom takes, blesses and then, in return, feeds them from this Loaf, defining how each person nourishes and strengthens the others.

The Cup of Blessing

"My Cup Overflows" [Psalm 23:5]

During the Passover Meal (the Seder), four cups of wine represent the four acts of deliverance promised by God in Exodus 6:6-7:

> "I will bring out"
> "I will deliver"
> "I will redeem"
> "I will take"

The third cup is known as "the Cup of Blessing" or "the Cup of Redemption," where we bless, thank and praise the great Redeemer Who has released His People from their slavery – and even more so for Christians, who are being blessed far more richly than we could ever dream of as He gives His very own Self to us!

"This is My Blood of the Covenant" [Matthew 26:28; Mark 14:24]

> For the life* of the flesh is in the Blood; and I have given it to you on the altar to make atonement for your lives*; for, as life*, it is the Blood which atones for the life* ... For the life* of every creature is its Blood.
> Leviticus 17:11, 14   [*"Soul" or "Life"]

More than just a liquid, Blood is the very essence of Life, the Soul of the individual. But this is not just any Blood, this here is *God*'s Blood. An awesome spinoff of the Incarnation is that for the first time in history, GOD HAS BLOOD! – He has Blood to give, He has Life to give, His very Soul He would share. In receiving Jesus' Blood, it now is GOD'S Life that flows in our veins.

> The root-idea of this rite of blood-friendship [Blood Covenant] seems to include the belief, that the blood is the life of a living being; not merely that the blood is essential to life, but that, in a peculiar sense, it is life; that it actually vivifies by its presence; and that by its passing from one organism to another it carries and imparts life. The inter-commingling of the blood of two organisms is, therefore, according to this view, equivalent to the inter-commingling of the lives, of the personalities, of the natures, thus brought together; so that there is, thereby and thenceforward, one life in the two bodies, a common life between the two friends: a thought which Aristotle recognizes in his citation of the ancient proverb: "One soul [in two bodies]," a proverb which has not lost its currency in any of the centuries.
> H. Clay Trumbull[51]

This is Blood-transfusion as Life-transfusion in all its fullness!

"This cup which is poured out for you ..." [Luke 22:20]

> For Jehovah's portion is His People, ... He encircled him, He cared for him, He kept him as the "apple" of His eye. ... he ate the produce of the field ...with the fat grains of wheat – and of the blood of the grape you shall drink wine.   Deuteronomy 32:9-10, 14

As a representation of Blood, fresh grape juice/wine is ideal. The color from the red grape is evocative of Blood. The juice is active, alive, because of which it alters into wine, constantly changing. Sadly, the grape juice of today has been sterilized – its life has been killed, which spoils its symbolism of imparting life. And obviously, plain water just does not cut it here.

With its overtones of deliverance, it is not by accident that Jesus would have chosen this third cup of wine in the Seder, the Cup of Redemption/Blessing, to be the pivot of His sharing His Life with us. Not merely a bottle of wine, the Blood of Jesus is not only connected with His death, but it contains all the Life of God in one sip.

One

> For just as the bread is made out of many grains ground and mixed together, … each grain loses its form and body and takes upon itself the common body of the bread; and just as the drops of wine, in losing their own form, become the body of one common wine and drink – so it is and should be with us, if we use this sacrament properly. Christ with all saints, by his Love, takes upon himself our form [Phil. 2:7], fights with us against sin, death, and all evil. This enkindles in us such Love that we take on his form, rely upon his righteousness, life, and blessedness. And through the interchange of his blessings and our misfortunes, we become one loaf, one bread, one body, one drink, and have all things in common. O this is a great sacrament, says St. Paul, that Christ and the church are one flesh and bone. Martin Luther[52]

A loaf of Bread: the Body of Christ is the active mutual oneness of the Bride with Her Beloved. A bottle of Wine: the Blood of Jesus unites His Bride in the very Life of God. And "Thou" – us and the Lord. In joy. In delight. In intimacy. Forever.

11. The Bride Responds

Maranatha!
Oops – There's the Doorbell!

(Scene 1)

Startled, the wife goes over to the window, and sees cars up and down the block, security personnel standing at key points around the house. In total dismay, the wife exclaims, "It is the King! Whatever shall I do? The house is not spotless! I do not have any crumpets for tea!"

(Scene 2)

Startled, the wife goes over to the window, and is pleased to see her husband standing at the door, "Oh, it is my Beloved!" (so what that he also happens to be the King!). Eagerly she runs toward the door (you know, *newlyweds*).

What if Jesus rang the doorbell and was standing on our doorstep? How would we react? As if it were a formal occasion, at which we panic, concerned whether we have prepared enough, cleaned enough; whether all is in order, "just perfect"? Or would it be the joy of the Bride running to meet her Beloved?

The King's Attitude

Will He walk in the door and first inspect the premises with white gloves to see if it is worthy of Him? Or will He rejoice, His focus being on in the Bride running to meet Him? This is the Bride that He has taken from the gutter, whom He Himself has washed and made beautiful. She is His great joy and delight [Psalm 16:3; Isaiah 62:5]. Should there be a smudge on His Beloved's cheek, He tells her to hold still a moment as He gently wipes it away; or if her feet be dirty, *He* will kneel and wash her feet in His forgiveness [John 13:3-15] – a necessary but merely incidental task, because He has come not for the blemish but for the Bride.

After all, this is His Beloved! He wants her radiant beauty to unmistakably shine forth, because His thought is not on Himself but on her:

Just as the Son of Man did not come to be served, but to serve …
Matthew 20:28

The Bride's Reaction

The Bride knows where she comes from. She also knows the route that has taken her to be where she is now. But she also knows that she is not on probation. It is not that kind of relationship. It is not a contract. It is not a master-servant, employer-employee relationship.

The Bridegroom does not have to "discover" what His Bride is really like. He has always known exactly what she would be like. Yet He still chooses her. Yet He still washes her. Yet He still leads her to His banquet. He has pledged Himself. God has backed Himself into a corner – on purpose. His Love is a wonderful and deliberate security.

She knows this – indeed "There is no fear in the Love [*agape*]; but perfect Love casts out the fear" [I John 4:18].

She Celebrates
The Eucharist

The Bridegroom in His joy has richly poured out extraordinary gifts: His Bride has gone from rags to the palace, made spotless and beautiful by His washing of water and the Word. The Father seats her on the throne by her Beloved's side for all eternity. And so much more!

The Bride, in deep and overwhelming gratefulness, responds in celebration:

I will greatly rejoice in Jehovah, my soul shall exult in my God; for *He* has clothed me with the garments of salvation, He has put on me the robe of righteousness, as a bridegroom wears a festive turban, and as a bride is adorned with her jewels. Isaiah 61:10

Let us rejoice and jump for joy and give the Glory to Him, since the marriage of the Lamb is come, and His Wife has made herself ready.
Revelation 19:7

The result is the Eucharist, an ancient Greek word describing Christian worship: it combines "good" (eu) and "benefit, grace, gift" (charis) ("Good Gift" – Jesus' part), and as a single word means "thanksgiving, gratefulness" (the Bride's response).

The Preface

At this Wedding Feast with our Beloved – indeed, "the Lord is with us!" – the Bride cannot help but lift heart and spirit in abundant, praiseful, grateful thanks in the pure joy of greeting the Bridegroom Who has come to give Himself to her yet once again. This is reflected in the Preface, a many-centuries-old part of the worship, which sets the tone for the day's celebration:

P/ The Lord be with you!
C/ And also with you![53]

P/ Lift up your hearts!
C/ We lift them to the Lord!

P/ Let us give thanks to the Lord our God!
C/ It is right to give Him thanks and praise!

P/ It is truly good, right, and salutary that we should always and everywhere thank You, holy Lord, almighty Father, everlasting God, [but chiefly are we bound to praise You for the glorious Resurrection of Your Son, Jesus Christ our Lord; He is the very Paschal Lamb offered for us, which has taken away the world's sins; Who by His death destroyed death and by His rising to life again restored to us everlasting life.]* Therefore, with angels and archangels and all the company of heaven we laud and magnify Your glorious Name, evermore praising You and singing:

C/ Holy, holy, holy Lord, God of pow'r and might: Heaven and earth are full of Your glory. Hosanna, Hosanna, Hosanna in the highest. Blessed is He Who comes in the Name of the Lord. Hosanna in the highest.

*(this changes to match the week's theme, here: Easter)

The Sacrifice of Praise

Our Sacrifice

Our prayer is really the Holy Spirit's witness with our spirit [Romans 8:15-17], likewise our good works "God prepared beforehand, that we should walk in them" [Ephesians 2:10], therefore

> In everything, whatever you do in word or work, do in the Name of the Lord Jesus, giving thanks to God the Father through Him.
> Colossians 3:17

> through Him, we should offer up a sacrifice of praise in all things to God, that is, the fruit of lips that jointly profess His Name.
> Hebrews 13:15

Our gratitude, praise and thanksgiving are essential in the Bride's response to the wonders of our Bridegroom's Love, in which His happiness is her central focus:

> I will praise God's Name with a song; I will magnify Him with thanksgiving. This will please Jehovah more than an ox or some young bull with horns and hoofs.   Psalm 69:30-31
>
> He whose sacrifice is thanksgiving glorifies Me; he who appoints his way, I will show him the salvation of God!   Psalm 50:23

"None shall come before me empty-handed," God had said [Exodus 23:15; 24:20; Deuteronomy 16:16]. The sacrifices of praise and thanksgiving are those special gifts He desires, which the Bride can always afford and which she does bring to her Beloved.

The Source of Our Sacrifice

In a "For Better or For Worse" (by Lynn Johnston) comic strip, Ellie and the kids are gone on a visit, so her husband John is "bach-ing" it for a while. His friend is eager about going out to enjoy the night life, but John simply wants to go home. His friend is surprised, "Don't you want to see how the single man lives?"

"I know how the single man lives," is John's reply, "that's why I got married!"

To his friend, John is making a "sacrifice."

But John is simply acting according to his appreciation for his relationship with his wife and family. It is not some dull, unenthusiastic chore – it is actually a response of gratitude, a response that rises out of his commitment to them. In worship, we "sacrifice" – or do we? It is simply acting from a different attitude, a different perspective: a heart of gratitude, a commitment of Love.

"Through Him ... Offer a Sacrifice of Praise" [Hebrews 13:15]

> To be sure this sacrifice of prayer, praise, and thanksgiving, and of ourselves as well, we are not to present before God in our own person. But we are to lay it upon Christ and let him present it for us ... we learn that we do not offer Christ as a sacrifice, but that Christ offers us.
>
> Martin Luther[54]

In the Old Testament, a person who is too poor to offer an animal, could offer a grain/flour sacrifice, but only as it "piggy-backed" on another's animal sacrifice (Leviticus 5:12). The Bride is destitute, in the gutter, when the Bridegroom finds her, washes her, and presents her to Himself without spot or shadow of sin. It is His sacrifice, and His alone, that opens the door to the Father, that opens the door to the Wedding Feast. Without this, there is no foundation for whatever she might bring in worship. Her sacrifices of prayer, praise, and thanksgiving can only be "thrown on top of" God's chosen Sacrifice, Jesus Christ, and only then can her gifts please the Father – *and they do please Him*!

The Security of His Love

She Repents

Standing now in the presence of her Beloved, the Bride feels sadness and disappointment, even revulsion, at her sin – but there is no fear. The Bridegroom's utter commitment "now and forever" – not just "till death do us part" –, gives her the courage to expose even the hidden things, the secret things, the things she is too ashamed to let anyone else see.

It is the risk of in essence saying, "This is who I really am – can You still Love me?"

This Spouse responds with, "I have known about that already for a long time – from even before the world was created! And I have Loved you with an everlasting, Steadfast Love all this time."

What a shock to realize "That of which I am so ashamed has not prevented the Beloved from loving me. That which I am so desperate to hide has not made me rejected. That secret that I am so afraid might get out has not made me unlovable." In humility and wonder the message is that "I really am Loved – really!

The Mutual Joy of His Forgiveness

It can be bewildering. The Beloved could use this knowledge of her faults, failures, and mistakes against His Bride, putting her down and manipulating her, and yet He never does. Instead she discovers that absolutely nothing changes in His Love: He still leads her in great joy by the hand to the Wedding Feast. His message is, "I have washed the blemish and it is gone – I no longer even remember it [Hebrews 8:12; 10:17]. I am so glad that now you are free of this. My Love has not diminished – in fact, we now share even greater Love with this one less barrier in our relationship." The presence of the Bridegroom brings peace and joy to the Bride, literally freeing her from her past.

Real Participation

"In Remembrance of Me" [Luke 22:19; I Corinthians 11:24, 25]

A day is set aside each year to remember those who gave their lives in various wars....

In a test we are called upon to remember a fact, whether it has any usefulness to us or not....

We wistfully recall a notable experience that is long past....

– are these the kind of remembrance that Jesus is talking about?

A variety of words take on new definitions and new life at the hands of the New Testament writers. For example, the Greek "Agape," once a little used word, becomes filled with an extraordinary depth, now having the meaning of the total, 100% self-giving Love of the Bridegroom for His Bride. So also is the word for "remembrance" changed in the Bible.

Vivid Memory

The word in the Greek is *anamnesis* (good luck trying to pronounce it!). Beyond the idea of reminiscing, it speaks of where one literally relives an event. Remember that embarrassing situation – the one where you re-agonize, almost moment by moment, over it all again? There is a sense of being present once more at that event. In fact, sometimes your body responds in a similar way as back then (stomach churns, and so forth).

However, this "remembrance" – *anamnesis* – goes even a step farther. Instead of an event that comes from the past to you in the present, this is a phenomenon that draws you back into the original event, in which you now participate, despite that you yourself were not around when it first happened. Perhaps an example would be helpful:

> And, so to speak, through Abraham, also even Levi, who receives tithes, paid tithes for he was still in the loins of his father when Melchizedek met him. Hebrews 7:9-10

Levi is a couple of generations removed from when Abraham gave the tithe to Melchizedek, yet Hebrews declares that he *participates* in the event – not as an action that occurs *in Levi's lifetime*, not that he would be continuing or repeating this action, but rather that he *participates* in *that original event* that happened those many years earlier.

An interesting corollary in this regard is the Hebrew word *zakar* (remember) for the circumcised male child:

> The word is used of males who are participants in the rite of circumcision {Gen 17:10; 34:15 Ex 12:48 etc.} and frequently connotes male persons of the Israelite society who were counted in censuses.
> TWOT[55]

Why use "remember" to describe the circumcised person? It is because his circumcision is not an isolated event but rather it participates in, and continues, the circumcision by which Abraham enters Covenant [Genesis 17:10; see 34:15; Exodus 12:48]. This same root word provides the Old Testament version of "remembrance" (*zeker* [for example, Exodus 3:15; Psalm 30:4; 34:16]) and "memorial" (*zikkarôn* [for example, Exodus 12:14; 13:9; 28:12,19]).

Celebrating the Passover

Another illustration of this sense of "remembrance" is the celebration of Passover. Passover is when the Lord does powerful signs and wonders in Egypt which culminate in the Angel of Death bringing death to the firstborn of man and beast. By entering through the Blood of a Lamb (the Blood is smeared on the posts and lintel of the door to the house), the Israelite is saved from that death. Following this "salvation," again by mighty wonders, Israel leaves Egypt, eventually to enter the Promised Land.

Every year the Israelite, now Jew, holds a *remembrance* of Passover. But it is no mere recalling of a dusty old event. Rather the Jew sees himself, so to speak, as actually being there in Egypt in the loins of his ancestor. He sees himself as an active participant in this salvation.

> *He* is huddled in the house, hearing the cries of anguish arise in the land;
> *he* is there eating in haste, prepared to depart at a moment's notice;
> *he* is there with new life beckoning to him
> – *he* is there *witnessing* the mighty deliverance of God.

There is a collapsing of time – it toys at the very fringes of eternity. *Anamnesis* is not a memory you recall, but one that draws you into the event itself.

At Table with the Bridegroom

So also Communion. The culmination of "Maranatha! – He comes!" is that the Bride actually sits at Table with her Beloved: there, at that first time back in the Upper Room; here, in this community of the faithful; and soon, in the great house of God the Father on the Last Day – all one event, all the same event. He is speaking directly to *her* when He says that with great earnestness He has earnestly desired to have this meal with her. He is speaking directly to *her* when He says, "Take eat, this is My Body... Drink of it all of you, this is My Blood."

We are that Bride, as every Christian has been, and every Christian to come will be. As one Body, we have been drawn back to that first Supper, to live in that event. *It* is not repeated – rather we are included. We now sit among Peter, John, James, Thomas – and all the saints of all time.

Eavesdroppers?

Sadly, over the many centuries, we seem to have gotten away from this powerful concept. When the Sacrament is consecrated, we seem to act as if the words, "This is My Body… This is My Blood," are addressed specifically to the Bread and Wine. The focus of concentration seems to be on these physical elements, while the people are almost treated as eavesdroppers.

But if we are indeed at the Table when the Lord first said these words, then He is looking *us* in the eye as He lifts the Bread and the Cup. It is not to the physical elements He is speaking, but to *us*. Perhaps the officiant should come to the very rail and look his congregation in the eye when he repeats these words so that the participants understand that it is indeed to them that the Bridegroom is speaking.

The reality of this event depends primarily upon the presence of the Bridegroom – but also upon the presence/remembrance of the Bride, because the Bridegroom has connected these presences.

The Whole Thing

To the Jew, the Passover celebration does not merely indicate participation in the meal, but rather that it is the center of a whole "salvation" event, and therefore it represents a participation in all of it, from the first plague to the entrance into the Promised Land. So also this Supper is the focus of God's climactic "salvation" event – as quoted previously:

> For the preaching ought to be nothing but an explanation of the words of Christ when He instituted [Holy Communion] and said: "This is my body, this is my blood," etc. What is the whole gospel but an explanation of this testament? Christ has gathered up the whole gospel in a short summary with the words of this testament or sacrament.
>
> Martin Luther[56]

And as St Paul captures the same idea:

> For as often as you eat this Bread and drink the Cup, you proclaim [announce, declare, make known] the Lord's death until He comes.
>
> I Corinthians 11:26

As rich and powerful as the Communion event by itself can be, still it is only a focal point of the much larger salvation event that begins with the Bridegroom leaving His Father (the first Christmas), leaving His mother, wooing His Bride, dying for His Bride, rising again, and returning on the Last Day to take His Bride to her new and permanent home. More than merely reminiscing, Communion brings us inside the mighty acts of God's saving Love.

At a Loss for Words

To Sleep, Perchance to Dream…

In the assisted living residence where this writer worked as chaplain, the hairdresser's shop was next to his office. One day as she wheeled out a resident who was fast asleep, she said, "See, I even put them to sleep!"

His rueful response was, "Yeah, I do, too."

Now be careful! It is fun to rib preachers about long sermons, dull sermons, sermons that could rival lead for sheer dead weight. But you may just have *your* day as well.

Look Who's the Preacher Now!

Again: "For as often as you eat this Bread and drink the Cup, you proclaim [announce, declare, make known]…" [I Corinthians 11:26] – "*you proclaim*" – welcome to the league of preachers! See, you were told to be careful! Of course, you may be very thankful that at least your sermon is without words. And it is short, sweet, and complete: your sermon is in your action. Do you realize how good a preacher you are, much less that you are a preacher? So, now, what are you preaching? Well, actually it is a message with multiple emphases, a message that the rest of the worship service illustrates in greater detail.

The Statement of Need

St Paul refers to the primary message in the above passage: "you proclaim the Lord's death." How that happens is because you have come to where Holy Communion is. Simply put, as every good sermon must, you start out with a statement of need: "I need what is to be found *here*." If we do not have this need, then we would be at the baseball game, or skiing, or whatever.

One criticism outsiders have of the Church is that it is full of sinners. And that is good – at least they have the first part of the message: sinners come here for what they need. But why *here*? Because what is to be found here is a marvelously complete solution – God's solution to sin.

The Lord's Death

We are not sent away with a new, or the old, Ten Commandments, a list of things to do, or a bunch of moralisms. Instead we encounter the Body that was broken on the Cross, the Blood that was so richly poured out, where Jesus paid in full the penalty that our sins demand.

But this is not merely a generic blanket solution! It is very personal and intimate: Jesus in Person touches each one of us, touches our lips, our bodies, our hearts – each individual, one at a time –, with His very Self, with His own Body and His own Blood. This is for *my* sins, for *your* sins, not just the generic "ours."

Let Go

Communion demands a decision from each one of us: on one hand Jesus stands with the fullest forgiveness there ever can be for every single sin. On the other hand are our sins – you know, even those sins we have spent a lot of time and effort nurturing, petting, feeding. Some have become pretty convenient for us. What shall we do then with them?

There is a warning for us: In Isaiah 38:17, we are told, "for You have thrown all my sins behind Your back." When Jesus died, God did that: thrown behind His back. After all, He does not want them around cluttering up His relationships with us, not even their carcasses. But what happens if we refuse to let go of those sins which He throws away? We will not enjoy the trip. Therefore, as we stand before Jesus, we are urged to repent – turn away, let go – of our sin. Our "sermon" then is to declare our determination to do just that as we come forward to the holy Lord Himself.

He Comes

We have help. Jesus once told a parable [Matthew 12:43-45] about an unclean spirit going out of a man, wandering around and then finally returning to the man and finding where he had stayed "tidy, swept, *and empty.*" Then when the unclean spirit gathers seven other spirits as roommates, Jesus remarks that the last state of that man is worse than the first. The key here is "empty." Even nature abhors a vacuum. Something that is empty wants to be filled.

Fortunately, that's why we come to the altar! Jesus comes here to us, enters and fills us with Himself. Wherever there is Jesus, there is no room for sin or Satan.

Until He Comes

Yet again:

> For as often as you eat this Bread and drink the Cup, you proclaim [announce, declare, make known] the Lord's death until He comes.
> I Corinthians 11:26

St Paul also refers to when Jesus comes on the Last Day to take us home – and that too is part of our proclamation: Jesus is in charge and the ultimate victory will be His – we have the down payment, the foretaste, of that glorious event here in the victory feast in this Supper. Our Communion and our lives have an unmistakable direction: ultimate eternal Communion at the Wedding Feast in heaven.

More to the Death

But there is more here than just (!) the forgiveness of sins. The Cross is so much more. Here is the evidence of the extraordinary self-giving Love of God. This is the backbone to all that has been discussed about the joy and eagerness of God in Communion, His utter delight in the Beloved.

Communion is the culmination and satisfaction that stems out of the Love that has made the Cross a reality. Communion is proof that the Cross of Jesus is more than merely (!) a death. If that's all it is, end of story, it would have faded into the backdrop of many, many other deaths [I Corinthians 15:14, 17].

But the Resurrection now gives us the ability to celebrate, to proclaim Communion, to declare all the benefits and blessings which come from Him Who died, Who now lives, Who shares Himself totally, individually, powerfully, lovingly with each of us.

Now No Condemnation

In fact, this Sacrament is the repeated confirmation of Romans 8:1: "There is therefore now no condemnation for those who are in Christ Jesus."

If there is even the slightest condemnation still left, then Jesus would have to come in judgment as the holy Judge Who visits wrath upon sin. We would not survive even one Communion, when God – God the Son – personally comes to touch each of us and our lives.

The very fact that Communion can happen is the witness that "There is therefore now no condemnation…" No wonder we can return to our seats with joy! The simple act of going to Communion is indeed a most eloquent sermon in regard to our need and our Savior's answer of forgiveness and Life eternal! And just think, this took longer to describe than you did to preach it. Pretty neat! (And no one fell asleep in *your* proclamation!)

What a wonderful thing the Eucharist is as we celebrate and declare the presence of our Beloved with all that He brings into our lives within the great interchange of Love between Bridegroom and Bride.

12. The Liturgy

The Rehearsal

Worship is more than merely a ritual – it is also a rehearsal. But this is not merely practicing where we stand and sit, and what we will say or sing. The words of the Preface point out "It is truly good, right, and salutary that we should always and everywhere thank You, …" Weekly we practice together the attitudes, perspectives and actions that make up a Christian's daily life in the world.

Here we practice – and live – our wonderful relationship with Jesus: we see Him fulfill His promises; we see Him give Himself totally to us; we see Him in those who surround us; we practice a lifestyle of His presence and of thanksgiving.

When the service ends, none of this is over. Now we get to see how it works in our daily life. Now we test in deed what we learned, what we confessed, what we practiced. Gratitude and thanksgiving are the keynotes of our conduct, and the Bridegroom's joy seeps into our attitudes.

Leitourgia

Background of the Term

Ancient Greece did not have the municipal bureaucracy we have today. They did not have a paid public works department and all the rest. Their type of taxation encouraged a sense of ownership of the city. Depending on ability, one contributed his service in some way to help the community at large function properly: he might assist in building a public building or by helping dig a well; a sculptor might create a statue to beautify the public square; another might help in the political affairs of the city-state.

This was their *Leitourgia* – Liturgy –, from *laos* (people) and *ergos* (work; labor), the "work of the people for the common welfare." Borrowing the words from President Abraham Lincoln's Gettysburg Address, this was a service done "of the *people*, by the *people*, and for the *people*."

The Common Service

"Common" can mean "the usual, the ordinary" – some might even say, "the dull." But here it means "together" – a joint activity of God's People. And, of course, "Service" comes from the verb "to serve."

> ... I am among you as the One Who serves.   Luke 22:27

The Bridegroom has set the atmosphere:

> Jesus ... rose from supper, laid aside His garments, and wrapped Himself with a towel. Then He poured water into a basin, and began to wash the disciples' feet ... When He had washed their feet, taken His garments, and was reclining again, He said to them, "Do you know what I have done to you? You call me the Teacher and the Lord; and you are right, for I am. If therefore I, the Lord and the Teacher, washed your feet, you also ought to wash one another's feet, for I have given you a pattern, that as I did to you so also you should do.   John 13:1-5; 12-15

The Universe's Majesty, Almighty God, is on His knees in menial service to His creatures – actually not an uncharacteristic activity for Him Who must daily feed, clothe, pick up after us, and straighten out our messes.

As the Bride follows her Beloved's lead, no wonder her "Liturgy" is described as a "Common Service" – a "service" together (Him and us) both to her Lord and to each other.

Point/Counterpoint Surrounding Holy Communion

The Bridegroom comes to serve and to feed His Bride; she offers herself and her world to Him. He pronounces forgiveness, speaks His Love to her, shares His very Self; she is filled with adoration, as she honors, praises, and speaks her heart to Him. He gives her the most solemn pledge of His presence in her life as possible: His very own Body and Blood go with her back into the world. In response, she leaves determined to be His Bride always and in everything, living her life to His glory.

When mutual "service" is the keynote of Christian worship, how totally inappropriate is the comment, "I didn't get much out of it." That comment's self-centered nature is lethal to any marriage and to mutual "service." The concern is rather, "What have I put into it?" and "What can I do to please my Beloved and strengthen His Body?"

"Love One Another as I Have Loved You" [John 13:34; 15:12]

One Another

Earthly "communion" is something we have with our friends: we go out for a cup of coffee, play a round of golf, have a party. That they are our friends depends on whether they agree with us, whether we like them, whether we have common interests.

But THIS Communion means: through Jesus we have Communion with ALL who are in the Bride. It does not matter whether we like them, or that they agree with us, or even that we can stand them. It does not matter whether *we* approve of their dress code, personal grooming, attitude grooming, theological grooming, work ethic, ... We practice God's Love for each one.

Love

Jesus, stripped to the waist, told us all, "If I then, your Lord and Teacher, have washed your feet, you also ought to wash one another's feet" [John 13:14]. That is, "as I have Loved the Bride, washing her, making her beautiful, forgiving her, withholding not even My life from her, cleansing her, sharing Myself totally with her – this Bride that I have lifted from the gutter to the very heights of heaven – Love one another as I have Loved you."

We cannot come to Communion to be "alone with God."

In this "Common Service" we work together: confessing our faith together, speaking God's Word to each other, praying for one another, praising God with one voice, receiving each other's confession, forgiving one another, giving of our means, firming each other's confidence, strengthening and upholding each other before the Lord – and by this, we are learning to Love each other and to serve together.

My Brothers

> In as much as you did it to one to one of the least of these My brothers, you did it to Me.   Matthew 25:40

When Jesus says, "My brothers" – well, here they are! HERE in the "Common Service" is a concrete reality to these words:

> In that day you will know that I am in My Father, and you in Me, and I in you. John 14:20

Inescapably, if we are to serve Jesus, we must also serve each other. Our "Common Service" is the beginning point, the obvious and natural opportunity to do just that.

> For where two or three are gathered in My Name, there am I in the midst of them. Matthew 18:20

He is in our midst because He is IN us – we do not call Him down, rather HE calls us together, to be His People, His Church, His Bride. He is not just in everyone else; that same Jesus Who washed His disciples' feet is in you and me. That is what empowers us!

How Can I ... ?

In Theory

The Bride and her worship provide the practice arena – the training ground – where we learn how to treat one another, how we should act in our lives, how we may "Love one another" and thereby do exactly what the Bridegroom is talking about for everywhere else in our lives.

Or so goes the theory. But we have those people "whom we love dearest when they are farthest from us." We may even have "few" enemies, but those who are, have *earned* that distinction: they have done something terrible enough to us that they have graduated into this category.

Theoretically we should Love them. But the old heart just will not kick start. So now what?

"He Said So!"

Remember how faith is defined as taking God at His Word – "He said so"? Let's add one more item to the "How do you know…" list:

How do you know that you Love? Because He said so.

Whoa! What? Even if I do not feel Love, in fact quite the opposite?? Definitely! *Because He said so*:

We Love because He first Loved us. I John 4:19

not we should, we ought, we must, we could, we hope to, we might – just simply "we Love." If that's not enough, then there is always Romans 5:5:

> Hope does not humiliate us, because God's Love has been poured into our hearts through the Holy Spirit Who has been given to us.

We may feel hatred, apathy or whatever – it does not matter what we may *feel*. We are called upon to follow, to *believe*, not because we see it, but because *God* declares it. Which should we follow: our feelings or the Lord? Well, since HE said so, then *that* has to be the truth.

Well, Then, I Guess I Love

We Love. God said so. No embellishments or qualifications. Our task is not to make ourselves Love. Our task is not to make ourselves feel Love. Our task is not even to try to make ourselves want to Love. Our task is to act out the Love we have – the Love God says is already there, the Love He sees, already poured into our hearts.

Well, that is going to be hard. That will take some practice, in fact, a lot of practice! And such things cannot be done except as we actually rub shoulders with one another. Surprise! This is also why the Bridegroom has called us together – that's what the "Common Service" is all about! This is the place to try out our Love, test it, and develop it. That's our Liturgy.

The Midas Touch

A Most Startling Event

In those first centuries following Pentecost, the Bride was a group of people whose determined goal in life – their Liturgy – was to be that menial servant who washed other people's feet – because their Almighty Creator GOD did that! They did not accent great power and success; they did not dream of a glorious death in a "holy war"; they did not seek prestige and privilege; their model was the despised Cross, where not merely a Man but their *God* hung in disgrace and under a curse.

In the Bridegroom, the Bride encounters a Love far beyond anything else she has ever experienced. It gives her a strength and an attitude that would turn upside down what most people consider important and valuable. She will live as a servant, not to win points nor to manipulate, but simply to express a Love that she would literally die for.

Accountability

Evangeline Booth, the daughter of the founder of the Salvation Army, sat in a dirty slum cleaning the sores of a woman who was an addict living on the street. A friend, observing her, remarked, "I would not do that even if you paid me a million dollars!"

Evangeline simply replied, "Neither would I."

What has been difficult for the world to handle, is that here is a group of people who operate not from expediency, not from greed, not from power-grabbing, but from the simple question, "What would Jesus have me do?" It echoes into the nooks and crannies of the whole world: from the merchant to the king, from the parent to the professor, from the slave to the master, not merely "What would God have me do?" but rather "What would JESUS have me do? – this God-come-into-the-flesh, Who died because of His great Love even for His enemies, and Who washes *my* feet – what would Jesus have me do, 'to the least of these My brothers'?"

A Consciousness

The world has been changed by the Bride living with a different attitude and a new sense of accountability: out of the Christian environment such caring service as hospitals, orphanages, soup kitchens, the "Red Cross" have been born – born because there is a group who does it as to the Lord Himself [Matthew 25:34-40].

Even wars become accountable – starting with Thomas Aquinas' interpretation, the concept of a "just" war reaches new heights of moral and ethical responsibility, the result of the Bride who goes about asking constantly of herself, "What would Jesus have me do?" No longer does the attitude reign that the Lord simply supports us because He is *our* God – there comes a questioning whether a war, much less war crimes, can properly be justified before a *righteous* and *holy* Creator. After watching Israel go off into the Babylonian Captivity, there is an awareness that Jehovah will not necessarily support us when we are do things for the wrong reasons. Although we may be disappointed by some of the logic which has been presented through the centuries, still, that accountability in wars is even considered is noteworthy.

The concern for those in prison, for those who are the victims of crime, for those who are starving in Africa, for distant people fighting a cruel civil war – unmistakably, as people and nations now reach out to help, it has come from the influence of this sense of accountability. It is true in our modern times that many people, although so influenced, have no idea as *to Whom* they are to be accountable and why – but the Bride knows.

The Golden Mundane

The Bride lives out her accountability – her Liturgy – into daily life, where she seeks the touch of Bridegroom's redeeming Love in all things she encounters. Having stood on the very threshold of eternity, having clasped hands with Jesus and the vast company of heaven, standing on the mountaintop with a transfigured Body of Christ, she goes back into her usual life bearing something greater than the emptiness the world offers.

She goes, as it were, with a "Midas' touch" (Midas was the fabled king whose very touch turned everything to gold). The Bride has Jesus, and the Holy Spirit, and prayer – with these she touches, for example, something as common and ordinary as meal times, and, in the words of Peter Brunner, can through her table blessing

> extricate the food, which comes from God's good creation, from the sin-corrupted world and assign it to the new creation, in which all is very good again in Christ.[57]

The table prayer becomes an extension of the Bride's living out the Love of God, where eternity invades daily life and adds its characteristic stamp upon the ordinary things of this world. The eternal God, Father, Son and Holy Spirit, and God's People are now participants of even this mundane event of the day.

Tarnished Gold

A woman, helping for the first time, puts out the place settings for a congregational dinner. As Jesus has washed the feet of His disciples, this is her service to her Lord and to her congregation. This is part of her Liturgy. The mundane has been transformed. It is her gift to the Bridegroom of the Church.

A second woman without a word re-does all the place settings "correctly." She destroys the gift of the first woman – the gift given in service to her Lord. This is puzzling – why should the gift be thus destroyed? What is so important to so despise the first woman and her gift? Just who is it that is being served?

The first woman feels that she is considered inept, that her time and effort has been worthless, and therefore she never helps again.

Too easily the Liturgy of others can be overlooked, ignored, discarded or degraded. The Bride cannot afford to be content with the great power of the Liturgy being confined to the worship pews. It must proceed into the whole world of her Lord's People.

Packing a Lunch

Viaticum

Do you pack a lunch? How about including a bit of Bread and some Wine? "*Viaticum,*" loosely translated from the Latin, means, "On the way, with you." It refers to the lunch one would take along, especially on a journey, making it a "food for men wayfaring."

However, it also could refer to a travelling companion. In fact, "companion" has the same idea as "*Viaticum*" because the Latin "*cum panis*" means "with bread." And when we want to indicate and practice a fellowship, how often has food been an important element – a *shared* meal, and in many churches, often in the form of the traditional potluck.

Lunch For On the Go

"*Viaticum*" looks beyond the worship service, beyond the moment of Holy Communion. Its attention is turned to the Bride's continued "journey" in the world in the coming week. There is no surprise that when she is sent forth back into her usual life, the image of sustaining food would be included. This idea of "lunch for one on the go" is already present in the Old Testament Manna:

> For I do not want you to be ignorant, brothers, that our fathers were all under the cloud, and all passed through the sea, and all were baptized into Moses in the cloud and in the sea, and all ate the same spiritual food and all drank the same spiritual drink. For they drank from the

spiritual Rock which followed, and the Rock was Christ.

I Corinthians 10:1-4

And in the New Testament Manna:

> They said to him, "Therefore what sign do You do, that we might see, and believe You? What work will You do? Our fathers ate the manna in the wilderness; as it is written, 'He gave them bread from heaven to eat.'"
>
> Jesus therefore said to them, "Truly, truly, I say to you, it was not Moses who gave you the bread from heaven but my Father who gives you the true Bread from heaven, for the Bread of God is He Who comes down from heaven, and gives life to the world."
>
> They said to him, "Lord, always give us this Bread."
>
> Jesus said to them, "I am the Bread of Life; he who comes to Me shall never hunger, and he who believes in Me shall never thirst."

John 6:30-35

"Brown-Bagging It"

There was a time in the early Church where people would take home a piece of the Bread used in Holy Communion. The idea was so that every day they would continue the Communion from the Sunday – every day, as it were, they could go back to that time of fellowship and renew it; every day they could revitalize their spiritual connection to the Bridegroom.

It sounds like a pretty neat idea, but for some reason it did not last long. Possibly the potential for abuse was just too great. Rather than being used as the Lord had intended, the Bread may have begun to be something merely venerated – worshipped for and by itself.[58] But the Sacrament is not given to be an end in itself, it is only to be the means by which the Bridegroom comes to share Himself with His Bride – just the same as the words of institution that consecrate the Sacrament are never meant to be said to the Bread and Wine, but rather to the Bride – the participants. For despite the most holy purpose for which these elements are used, ultimately their only purpose ever is to be consumed ("take eat… take drink…"). It is Jesus entering us that is the focus, not merely that these elements are used.

"Go in Peace; the Lord is With You"

These words are the summation of the powerful, visible, physical confirmation of Holy Communion's spiritual reality. In the tangible, concrete eating and drinking, in this historical point in time, Jesus has definitely, specifically, really, irrevocably entered His Bride yet again.

All the participants have just had the astounding confirmation that it really is true: the Lord, the Bridegroom, is with us! Now as we step out into the world, just as truly as that Bread and Wine are now in our body, soon to become permanently one with the body, so also is Jesus in us, and we in Him – and this too is permanent.

These words should never be treated as a mere rote mechanical dismissal!

For the Journey

When we take along a brown-bagged lunch, it is so that we may maintain our strength and ability in order to handle whatever we encounter on our journey. Holy Communion certifies that Jesus now comes along, that we may know that indeed we have what it takes to handle whatever we encounter on life's journey. We have His Love, forgiveness, hope, strength, presence, abundant life, His pledge that all works together for our good, and so, so much more – all guaranteed by this experience at this Table. How could we not go in peace!

Perhaps according to our logic we should need this only once in our whole lives, but thank God He does not deal with us according to our logic! He loves to constantly share Himself with us, especially in this way. It is such a joyous time for Him – He earnestly looks forward to this time of sharing, He rejoices over us "as a Bridegroom rejoices over His Bride" (Isaiah 62:5). It is *our* delight to have Jesus with us, our jubilation to have Him share with us, and we with Him – and it is *His* delight.

On this journey, this is "Lunch" the Bride can take with her every day, by which her Bridegroom will take the ordinary and transform it into the sacred, and will equip her as she puts "service" into what she has practiced in her worship.

13. He Is Known

The Emmaus Experience

Behold, two of Jesus' followers on that same [Easter] day were going to a distant village named Emmaus, about seven miles from Jerusalem, and they were talking with each other about everything which had happened. It was as they talked and debated, Jesus himself drew near and went with them, but their eyes were kept from recognizing Him. He said to them, "What are these words which you toss about between you as you walk?"

And they stopped, looking sad. One of them, named Cleopas, answered him, "Are You visiting Jerusalem and the only one who does not know the things that have happened in it in these days?"

He said to them, "What things?"

He said to Him, "The things concerning Jesus of Nazareth, Who was a man – a Prophet – mighty in deed and word before God and all the people, and how our chief priests and rulers delivered Him up to the judgment of death, and crucified Him. But we had hoped that it was He Who was about to redeem Israel.

"In addition, besides all these things, this is the third day since these things happened – and then some women of our company astonished us: they went early to the tomb and had not found His body; however they came claiming to have seen a vision of angels, who said that He was alive. Some who were with us went to the tomb, and found it just as the women had said; Him, however, they did not see."

He said to them, "O foolish ones, and slow of heart to believe all that the prophets have spoken! Was it not necessary for the Christ to suffer these things and to enter into His glory?" And beginning with Moses and all the prophets, He interpreted to them in all the Scriptures the things concerning Himself.

They drew near to the village to which they were going and He appeared to be going further. They urged Him, saying, "Abide with us, for it is toward evening and the day is nearly over."

So He went in to abide with them, and, as it was, He reclined at table with them, He took the Bread and blessed it, and having broken it, He gave it to them. And their eyes were opened and they recognized Him; and He vanished out of their sight. They said to each other, "Did not our hearts burn while He spoke to us on the road, while He opened to us the Scriptures?"

Rising up that same hour, they returned to Jerusalem and found the eleven and those with them gathered together, who said, "The Lord has risen indeed, and has appeared to Simon!" Then they described what had happened on the road, and how He was known to them in the Breaking of the Bread. As they were telling these things, He Himself stood in the midst of them ...   Luke 24:13-36

The Emmaus account is indeed a beautiful one. What a comfort the story gives – in the midst of heartache and sorrow, in the midst of despair and disillusionment, the Bridegroom personally comes to give joy and triumph to His Beloved. He walks with them, He goes to where they live, He lets them discover Him, He lets them see Him. He is known to them.

The Breaking of the Bread

Later, especially in Acts 2:42, Luke shows that the phrase "the Breaking of Bread" was the early Christians' name for Communion, being one of their significant actions of worship right from the beginnings of the Church.

> What is more, in the Gospels, where the first day of the week is linked inseparably with the resurrection of Christ, it is also linked with the assembly of the community [John 20:19,26] and with the meal of the community [Luke 24:28-35, 41-42; Mark 16:14; cf. John 21:1-14; Acts 10:41]. The crucified Jesus is known as Lord in the assembly; the one who was executed is known as risen in the breaking of bread....
>
> The Emmaus meal story...was told at least in part to interpret the current practice of the hearers' churches: the risen Lord is known in the community's Meal. That the substructure of this story (Word, Luke 24:25-27, and Meal, vss 28ff) and its setting on the evening of the first day of the week closely paralleled the meeting on the evening of the first day of the week in Acts 20 and that meeting's structure (Word, vs 7, and breaking of bread, vs 11) may be taken as evidence that the Emmaus account was told ... with intended and evident connection to every Sunday's meeting with its Word and Meal! There our hearts also burn at

his Word. There we too know him in the bread.

Gordon W. Lathrop[59]

He is Known

As these two Emmaus disciples recount the events of their afternoon – the climax being that Jesus is known in the Breaking of Bread – as they are sharing these things, He Who is the Resurrection stands among them. Now we also have the same opportunity. Every Sunday is meant to be a "little Easter" – again He comes to simply be among His Beloved, to speak of what He has done and is doing, to share His very self, to give joy and triumph. Every week He has come to where we live, He has touched us and we have touched Him. Again He is known to His Bride.

To Know Him Again

We have come to know Jesus "in the Breaking of Bread." Throughout these topics, we have watched Him as the Bridegroom, Who with indescribable joy and delight has brought His Beloved Bride to His Table in His willingness and eagerness to be at table every time Holy Communion is celebrated. And celebrated it is, by both God and Man; by Christ, both Head and Body.

We have glimpsed the Head as He has empowers His Body the Church. We have seen His daily presence and the peace that it brings. His Blood is Life and it now flows through our veins. What a beginning this has made. Let's go again to Bridegroom's Table, where again we may know Him in this Breaking of the Bread.

Endnotes

[1] Since the Hebrew for this word does not really specify "love," but its root refers to a shepherding context, its idiomatic sense may lean more toward a term of endearment.

[2] In this and related passages [Matthew 12:46-50; Luke 8:19-21], Jesus draws a contrast between His mother and brothers and those around Him, listening to Him. Why the contrast? Because His family is not there where He is teaching. Because they insist that He stop what He is doing and pay attention to their "more important" concerns. In fact, even His brothers, at least at this time, do not believe in Him [John 7:2-9], and "His own people ... said, 'He is out of His mind'" [Mark 3:21]. So Adam's prophesied break of the Son from His mother – and family – is indeed necessary as Jesus woos His Bride.

[3] Sometimes the little passages can have tremendous significance – of such is the case with Luke 2:21, when Jesus' circumcision is mentioned in passing and yet is really an amazing event: for the first time in the history of *the universe*, God actually has Blood to shed in Covenant.! Up to this point, Covenant has been one-sided: only the humans shed Blood (in Circumcision). Although Jehovah fully honors His commitment, still the relationship limps, since not being a physical Being, He has no Blood to contribute. However now, in Jesus' Circumcision, like an explosion, God's involvement by *His own Blood* travels throughout all time to connect with every godly Circumcision, and now every such Covenant relationship is complete.

[4] That God dies is the import of the Covenant ceremony in Genesis 15:8-12, 17 – the pledge as one passes through the split carcasses of the animals is that "If I break Covenant, then I will become like these carcasses." The prophecy of the breaking of this Covenant is found in Zechariah 11:10-14, where the setting of this occasion is established as when Jesus dies. More on Covenant can be found in this author's book *Covenant: The Blood is the Life*, available on Lulu.com and Amazon.com.

[5] In Greek, this is the root for the "fullness" in the previous verse.

[6] Referring to endnote 4 above, the idea of the split carcasses is that Covenant is represented by the living whole animal. Broken Covenant is like tearing the animal into two, while its Blood, Life, Soul drains away, leaving only dead remains behind.

[7] Berthold von Schenk, *The Presence* (New York: Ernst Kaufman, Inc., 1945), 41

[8] Fred H Lindemann, *The Sermon and the Propers* (Concordia Publishing House: St Louis, Missouri, 1958), 142.

[9] "For the life of all flesh is the Blood" [Leviticus 17:14] – the word translated as "life" is actually "soul," throughout this verse, as it is in verse 11, Genesis 9:4 and Deuteronomy 12:23; therefore Jesus really is giving us Himself "body and soul"!

[10] The traditions identified in these paragraphs are described in

http://www.wildolive.co.uk/weddings.htm and
http://www.oasistradepost.com/Weddings_/weddings_.html

[11] Not only does Jesus in His greatest distress cry out, "Abba, Father" [Mark 14:36], this familiar Name is also to be found on our lips as well [Romans 8:15; Galatians 4:6].

[12] Just as today, more and more want all the benefits of what God offers, meanwhile rejecting Him, His will and His solution to mankind's problems.

[13] Martin Luther, "The Babylonian Captivity of the Church," *Luther's Works (American Edition), Volume 36: Word and Sacrament II,* General Editors: Jaroslav Pelikan and Helmut T. Lehmann (Philadelphia: Fortress Press, 1959), 18. The cited source had a footnote: "In I Tim 3:16 Christ himself is called the *sacramentum* [Vulgate]."

[14] Martin Luther, "Sacrament of Holy Baptism," *Small Catechism.* Translation by Robert E. Smith from the German text, printed in: Triglot Concordia: The Symbolical Books of the Ev. Lutheran Church (St. Louis: Concordia Publishing House, 1921), 538-559. http://www.gutenberg.org/cache/epub/1670/pg1670.txt; retrieved March 13, 2012.

[15] This concept of timelessness and presence is discussed in "11. The Bride Responds," in the section "Real Participation" [page 130] where Levi is said to have paid tithes to Melchizedek, even though he was "still in the loins" of his great-grandfather Abraham [Hebrews 7:9-10]. It also is found in the Israelite/Jewish celebration of Passover, where they are "present and participating in" the original event, as "in the loins" of their ancestors.

[16] Martin Luther, "The Blessed Sacrament of the Holy and True Body of Christ, and the Brotherhoods," *Luther's Works (American Edition), Volume 35: Word and Sacrament I,* General Editors: Jaroslav Pelikan and Helmut T. Lehmann (Philadelphia: Mulenberg Press, 1960), 53

[17] His wife had died during the time when he was writing his book.

[18] von Schenk, 128-131

[19] Dr Martin H Scharlemann, *The Secret of God's Plan: Studies in Ephesians,* (Saint Louis, Missouri: Concordia Publishing House, 1970), 20.

[20] Apparently that is possible today: a company has made sealed packets of the wafer and the wine/grape juice, dubbed by some as the "MacWafer," to be distributed to communicants, so that one need not be tainted by fellow communicants and whatever "ick-i-ness" they may have.

[21] Bob Slosser, *Miracle in Darien:* (Bridge-Logos Publishers, January 1980); also http://www.cbn.com/spirituallife/BibleStudyAndTheology/TheHolySpirit/Renewal_Requires_Power_and_Guts_to_Succeed.aspx;

[22] But beware, there is a difference between "braying" and praying! [Luke 18:10-14]

²³ Luther, "Blessed Sacrament," 70.

²⁴ *Ibid*, 54, 57

²⁵ Martin Luther , "Confession And The Lord's Supper," from volume II:193-214 of *The Sermons of Martin Luther*, (Grand Rapids, MI: Baker Book House, 1983) as found on http://www.lectionarycentral.com/maundy/LutherEpistle.html, retrieved March 15, 2012.

²⁶ David Sargent, "A Messianic Passover Haggadah," http://www.godandscience.org/apologetics/haggadah.html. Retrieved 2012-04-23

²⁷ http://www.cgg.org/index.cfm/fuseaction/Library.sr/CT/BQA/k/221/Sop-Leavened-Unleavened-John-13-26-27.htm:

> We also need to understand the "sop" itself. This is the Greek word psomion, and means "a morsel," "a crumb," "a bit," "a fragment," or as Strong's interprets, "a mouthful." Thus, it means a piece of food, and in the Last Supper, one used particularly for dipping. Therefore, the word does not necessarily suggest that the sop was used for soaking up liquid. It could also be used like a potato or tortilla chip for dipping in a sauce or for scooping up smaller bits of another food toward the mouth.

²⁸ Jesus dies in 33 AD, when the Passover falls on a Saturday. Since no cooking is allowed on the weekly Sabbath, the Babylonian Talmud decreed that in such a situation, the death of the lambs would begin at 12:30 PM, so that the cooking might be finished before the Sabbath begins. (Pilate presents Jesus before the crowd at about noon, "the sixth hour" [John 19:14]; an half hour later, "the Lamb of God" is crucified.).

Since all days begin sundown the evening before, then "the Day of Preparation" has already begun when Jesus eats the Last Supper, although the Last Supper is still a day earlier than when the Passover meal is usually eaten.

²⁹ Martin Luther, "The Sacrament Of The Altar," *The Large Catechism* by Dr. Martin Luther; Translated by F. Bente and W. H. T. Dau, April, 1999; http://www.gutenberg.org/cache/epub/1670/pg1670.txt; retrieved March 13, 2012.

³⁰ Luther, "Babylonian Captivity," 73-74.

³¹ Martin Luther, "Receiving Both Kinds in the Sacrament," *Luther's Works (American Edition), Volume 36: Word and Sacrament II*, General Editors: Jaroslav Pelikan and Helmut T. Lehmann (Philadelphia: Fortress Press, 1959), 245.

³² Martin Luther, "Confession concerning Christ's Supper," *Luther's Works (American Edition), Volume 37: Word and Sacrament III*, General Editors: Jaroslav Pelikan and Helmut T. Lehmann (Philadelphia: Mulenberg Press, 1961), 367

³³ The Greek word here is the word used in the Septuagint translation of the Old Testament for the pleasing odor of when a sacrifice is offered according to God's way, for example, Genesis 8:21; Exodus 29:18, 25, 41.

[34] Martin Luther, "Treatise on the New Testament," *Luther's Works (American Edition), Volume 35: Word and Sacrament I*, General Editors: Jaroslav Pelikan and Helmut T. Lehmann: (Mulenberg Press: Philadelphia), 106

[35] Luther, "Both Kinds," 252

[36] Martin Luther, "The Misuse of the Mass," *Luther's Works (American Edition), Volume 36: Word and Sacrament II*, General Editors: Jaroslav Pelikan and Helmut T. Lehmann (Philadelphia: Fortress Press, 1959), 198.

[37] Theodore G Tappert, trans., *Book of Concord*, (Philadelphia: Fortress Press, 1959), 453.61

[38] Luther, "Babylonian Captivity," 49.

[39] *Book of Concord*, 453.61

[40] Luther, "Babylonian Captivity," 42

[41] Luther, "New Testament," 88-89.

[42] Luther, "New Testament," 87-88.

[43] Luther, "Babylonian Captivity," 46

[44] "pro" = "before"; "fane" = church – "profane" (from which we get "profanity"), is something that is done "before the church" or "in front of the church," which incidentally is also done in full view/awareness of the community.

[45] Luther, "In Conclusion," *Large Catechism*

[46] von Schenk, 45

[47] Luther, "New Testament," 91.

[48] *Ibid*, 104

[49] Martin Luther, "That These Words of Christ, 'This is My Body,' etc., Still Stand Firm Against the Fanatikcs" *Luther's Works (American Edition), Volume 37: Word and Sacrament III* (General Editors: Jaroslav Pelikan and Helmut T. Lehmann: Mulenberg Press: Philadelphia) , 127.

[50] Luther, "New Testament," 104

[51] H. Clay Trumbull, *The Blood Covenant: A Primitive Rite and Its Bearing on Scripture* (Reprint Publisher: Kirkwood, Mo.: Impact Christian Books, 1975), 38

[52] Luther, "Blessed Sacrament," 58.

[53] What is happening in this little interchange between pastor and congregation? The pastor blesses the people ("The Lord be with you!") and then, in return, *the people bless him* – especially "with your *spirit!*" which is the area of the pastor's dual function as

spokesman for God and spokesman for the people. This interchange often occurs in past liturgies before three significant actions: when the pastor "collects" the thought of the day in prayer; when he consecrates and distributes Holy Communion; and when he pronounces the benediction, the final blessing of the Liturgy.

[54] Luther, "New Testament," 99.

[55] R Laird Harris, *Theological Wordbook of the Old Testament*, vol I (Chicago: Moody Press, 1981), 243.

[56] Martin Luther, "Treatise on the New Testament," *Luther's Works (American Edition), Volume 35: Word and Sacrament I*, General Editors: Jaroslav Pelikan and Helmut T. Lehmann: (Mulenberg Press: Philadelphia), 106

[57] Peter Brunner, *Worship in the Name of Jesus* (St Louis, Missouri: Concordia Publishing House, August 1980), 294.

[58] This is what happened to "the Brass Serpent," which God commanded Moses to make to end the plague of serpents in Numbers 21:18-19. Originally it was a "sign" – one looked toward that which God provided according to His promise, and therefore received God's salvation. Jesus refers to this as the description of when He "is lifted up" [John 3:14], that by looking to God's solution on the cross, a person will be saved. Yet centuries later, in II Kings 18:4, rather than drawing one's attention to Jehovah, *the serpent* is now worshipped as a god itself.

[59] Gordon W. Lathrop, "Toward Doing the Confessions: The Lord's Supper on the Lord's Day," *Una Sancta* (Vol ?), pg s7

www.ingramcontent.com/pod-product-compliance
Lightning Source LLC
Chambersburg PA
CBHW031145160426
43193CB00008B/262